# GROWING UP
# IN
# 13TH CENTURY
# ENGLAND

Taking the 1270s as typical of the century, the author gives a realistic and detailed description of the everyday life of children in five English families of different social classes: that of an earl, a knight, a peasant, a London merchant, and a craftsman in an East Anglian town. There are three children in each family, two boys of fourteen and ten and a girl of twelve. In this lively and entertaining book, the author tells us about their schooling, their daily training for adult life, the different prospects for the elder and younger sons, and what kind of marriage the girls may expect.

Alfred Duggan's books are particularly distinguished for their accuracy and clarity of style. *Growing Up in 13th Century England* is an outstanding example of these qualities which have made the author so popular with readers of all ages.

# GROWING UP
# IN
# 13TH CENTURY
# ENGLAND

## ALFRED DUGGAN

*illustrated by C. Walter Hodges*

PANTHEON BOOKS

Second Printing

© Copyright, 1962, by Alfred Duggan

All rights reserved under International and Pan-American Copyright
Conventions. Published in New York by Pantheon Books, a Division
of Random House, Inc., and simultaneously in Toronto, Canada, by
Random House of Canada, Limited. Manufactured in
the United States of America.

First Published in Great Britain by Faber and Faber Ltd.
under the title "Growing Up in the Thirteenth Century"
Library of Congress Catalog Card Number: 62-15415

DESIGN: BETTY CRUMLEY

# INTRODUCTION

This book describes how young people lived in England seven hundred years ago. But because the 1260s were a time of civil war, when normal life was continually disrupted, I have described instead the more peaceful 1270s.

During the 1260s the struggle for power between King Henry III and the barons—the noblemen who held their lands directly from the King—reached its climax in the Barons' War. Simon de Montfort, Earl of Leicester and leader of the rebel barons, defeated King Henry at the battle of Lewes in 1263. The King and his son Edward were imprisoned, and Montfort, at the head of a barons' council, actually governed England for a year. But Prince Edward soon escaped to lead the royalist forces to victory at the battle of Evesham in 1264, where Montfort was killed. By 1267 all the barons had submitted to the King. In 1272 King Henry died and his son became King Edward I. It is he who is reigning during the more peaceful times described in this book.

Of course, the 1270s were not entirely peaceful; in the Middle Ages that would have been unnatural and perhaps not very much liked. But the wars of Edward I were fought outside his own kingdom, in Wales or Scotland, which was as it should be. The duty of a medieval king was to keep peace in his own land while making war on his enemies abroad. One reason for the unpopularity of the late King Henry III had been his inefficient conduct of the war against France, which went on more or less continuously as long as the King of England held land on the far side of the Channel.

The society of the thirteenth century was geared to war. For a large number of people warfare was the main business of life; complete peace, at home and abroad, would have left them without an occupation. What most men liked was a war going on somewhere, a long way off but not entirely out of reach; so that they could come back from the war in winter, or when they thought they had done enough fighting, and find their wives and families living in safety. For the second great duty of a king, after he had made war on his enemies, was to keep the peace among his own subjects. Edward I carried out both these duties with great success.

This book treats of the education of young people in its widest sense, the training of them for adult life as well as the book-learning taught to them; and because society in the thirteenth century was highly stratified, with little social contact between the great and the humble, it deals separately with the main social classes. But we must never forget that in the Middle Ages even the poorest peasant felt a sense of human dignity; he knew that the salvation of his soul was as important as the salvation of the King's soul, and that as a man he had rights and a duty to stand up for them. His social superiors knew it too, and knew that they could not push him too far.

# CONTENTS

INTRODUCTION  V

I  THE FAMILY OF AN EARL  3

II  THE FAMILY OF A COUNTRY KNIGHT  60

III  THE FAMILY OF A PEASANT  100

IV  THE FAMILY OF A RICH MERCHANT  133

V  THE FAMILY OF A CRAFTSMAN  179

# GROWING UP
## IN
## 13TH CENTURY
## ENGLAND

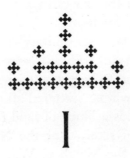

# I

## THE FAMILY OF AN EARL

In all England there were only a score or so of earls, and they were very great men. In the civil wars of Simon de Montfort's day the adherence of two or three earls to one side or the other made the difference between victory and defeat. An earl had to govern his estates with energy and competence, or someone would take them from him.

The earl who is the father of the children we will meet in this chapter seldom stays long in one place. For the great feasts of Christmas, Easter, and Pentecost he must show himself at the King's court; when the King goes to war he must ride with the army. Lesser men may avoid military service by paying scutage, the wages of a knight for the appropriate period. In fact the King prefers that they should offer money in place of service, since hired mercenaries are better trained, and more obedient to orders, than a crowd of country knights. But it is considered disgraceful that an earl should pay someone else to do his fighting for him.

In the intervals between military service and duty calls at court a sensible earl will visit every one of his estates at least once a year, to keep his tenants up to the mark; and these estates will be scattered all over England. Let us say that he holds a block of land in Sussex or Kent, which his ancestor received at the Norman Conquest; another block on the March of Wales, the frontier between Wales and England, won by the sword in the reign of William Rufus; and some valleys in the northern moors, the fruit of a prudent marriage during the twelfth century. If he follows the latest fashion he will have built a house beside the Thames, between the city of London and the village of Westminster, where he can lodge while he does business with the Exchequer. But perhaps one of his ancestors gave land to a monastery near London, which will forever afterward regard the whole family as benefactors; in that case he can lodge in the monastery and will have no need for a town house. When he goes to court, or visits London on business, he may take his countess with him; she will be eager to see the new modes from France and to meet other great ladies. But usually the children will stay at home.

Nevertheless, they will travel a great deal, because home itself will move with the seasons. The Yorkshire fief is for high summer, Sussex for winter; but late summer and autumn they pass in their great Welsh castle among the woods where their father has the right to hunt deer, which in his other woods are reserved for the King.

They will not travel in any wheeled vehicle. If you saw a knight riding in a cart you would assume that he was a prisoner on his way to the gallows. The Queen has a chariot, a long four-wheeled coach decorated with carving and tapestries; perhaps the Countess keeps one in the stable of the London house. But this luxurious wagon, covered with an embroidered canopy, is for use mainly on the cobbled streets of towns.

On journeys the poor walk, and everyone else rides. Unless there are enemies about, even a knight will not ride his war horse, which is always trying to bolt or to fight its neighbors; the French name for a war horse is "destrier," because it is normally led by the right, or "dexter," hand of a groom. Able-bodied knights ride hackneys, horses with a comfortable action and an appearance very like the modern hunter. Clerks, and the elderly, will ride mules, which have an even more comfortable action and never stumble on rough going. Ladies also ride hackneys or mules. When there is no hurry they sit sideways; though the sidesaddle has no horn for the right knee, so that the horse must be led by a man riding or walking at its head. But at a pinch, if enemies pursue or danger threatens, any lady can ride a destrier at full gallop. Then she must sit astride, her full wide skirts draped over the saddle to cover both legs. If she goes

CWALTER HODGES

hunting, which is a privilege reserved for very great ladies indeed, she will also ride astride.

To ride a destrier, with a lance in the right hand and a shield on the left arm, is a very difficult art; but every boy of knightly birth must learn it. It is said that a boy must be able to ride by the age of fourteen, or he will never learn properly. When little King Henry III rode to his coronation at the age of nine he was already an accomplished horseman. So Ralph, aged fourteen, will ride with the men, on a good hackney.

Anne, aged twelve, and Roger, aged ten, will ride astride on ponies. A well-mounted groom has been told to keep an eye on them, but they would feel insulted if he were to produce a leading rein.

When the children were smaller they traveled very comfortably, lying amid a nest of cushions in panniers slung on either side of a quiet baggage mule.

The Countess travels in a horse-litter. That is the most luxurious mode of transport, used by wealthy invalids and wounded knights. From the litter long shafts are attached to the packsaddles of horses before and behind. On a wide road you may use a litter borne by four horses, one to each shaft, and then the inside will be as roomy and comfortable as a modern railroad coach; but since these people are traveling on a Welsh hill road there is room for only one horse abreast.

In Wales there is always danger from raiders. The King's writ does not apply there, and every Marcher lord is responsible for the protection of his own property. So the travelers move with proper military precautions. First comes a group of spearmen and archers, Welshmen who hold their land by military service though they are not gentry; for in Wales every free man is a warrior. They ride common nags, but if they meet trouble they will dismount to fight. Their commander is one of the Earl's household knights, a young unmarried gentleman who serves for a wage and lives in the Earl's hall. He calls himself a knight bachelor, not so much because he is unmarried as because he is at the beginning of his career. He hopes that one day his lord will give him land to be held by knight service, or at least a position of trust, as seneschal or constable or castellan, in one of his castles. When he is thus provided for, he can marry and continue his noble family.

Behind the vanguard rides a clump of knights, either household bachelors or military tenants putting in the forty days of guard duty which they owe to their lord even in time of peace. Then, while the road is still not too trampled and muddy, come the Countess and her children.

At the back of the column is a similar rear guard; but before that an immense train of servants and baggage animals straggles along the road. The family are on their way to their Welsh castle for a stay of several weeks, and they take with them most of their movable possessions.

They bring all their clothes, of course, and all the horses they use for their own riding, their jewels, their armor, and their silver plate. They bring also some things that we would expect to find permanently in a country house: mattresses and bed linen, for example; great beds carefully taken apart to be carried on muleback; two or three armchairs with tapestry canopies; tablecloths and napkins; a great sack padded with raw wool in which a few books may travel without damage. The most unexpected baggage, in modern eyes, are a few mule-loads of stained-glass windows; their wooden frames can be fixed in the stone window-openings of the castle bedrooms to make them snug and windproof. Of course such windows cannot be opened, but there is never any lack of fresh air in a drafty castle. Glass is very expensive; even an earl cannot afford enough of it to keep a supply in all his houses. The glass of the thirteenth century is too full of bubbles and bumps to be properly transparent; but it lets in the light and keeps out the wind, and if it is adequately colored, the flaws are not obvious.

Besides the baggage animals, led by grooms, there are in the column dozens of attendants and servants, many of them mounted: chaplains, and writing clerks who are at least in minor orders; pages and squires who are young gentlemen; the huntsman and the falconer and the butler, who are upper servants of considerable dignity and might in some households be gentlemen also; austringers carrying hawks and kennel boys leading greyhounds, though the staghounds stay permanently in Wales because nowhere else may the Earl hunt deer; the chief cook, who, because he is clever with his fingers and accustomed to handling boiling water, is often called upon to dress wounds; and a crowd of common scullions and stableboys.

A considerable community is on the move. But every-one in it is used to traveling a dozen times or more in the year; they do it efficiently, without breaking anything fragile in the baggage. They are not traveling fast, for it does not much matter whether they reach their destination by nightfall. They carry food with them, and on some of the baggage animals are tents enough to shelter the whole party.

This time, however, they reach the Welsh castle before dark. The cooks at once go into action, preparing the meal they would have served by the roadside if the column had been delayed. Everyone has a hot supper and goes early to bed. Next morning the community in the castle will take up its usual late summer routine. The Earl is expected in a few days, as soon as he can get away from the King's army.

The morning begins very early, before sunrise. The days are already beginning to shorten and daylight must not be wasted. The ideal is for everyone to be up and dressed when the sun appears. This does not quite work out in practice, especially with the elderly and important. But children must do as they are told, and they tumble out of bed when the watchman on the tower blows his horn.

Ralph and Roger have shared a bed in the big upper room which shelters all the pages and squires, with a household knight sleeping by the door to keep order. Everybody gets out of bed stark naked (what the Middle Ages knew as nightgowns we should call dressing gowns).

The knight and a few of the older squires wear warm nightcaps, because drafts always blow through this long room with its unglazed windows; the younger boys trust to their hair to keep their ears warm.

Immediately everyone puts on a woolen shirt and woolen drawers. The men of the Middle Ages thought nakedness ugly and degrading; if they could see the sun-bathers on our modern beaches they would suppose that these holiday-makers were being forced to perform some humiliating punishment. Then the pages take their trestle beds apart, fold up the bedding, and place the whole thing neatly against the wall. But the squires and the two sons of the Earl leave this to the servants who will come in to clean up; though of course they could do it themselves if the castle were shorthanded in time of siege.

The bedding of the pages and squires, by the way, is rough and ready: mattresses and bolsters stuffed with straw, woolen blankets, perhaps a small linen pillow stuffed with wool, but certainly no linen sheets. Linen is an expensive material, nearly as costly as silk. The Countess has a pair of silk sheets for her great bed, and several changes of linen ones; instead of woolen blankets she has fur rugs. Ralph, as heir to the earldom, has one fur rug and a silk-covered pillow; they are among his most treasured possessions and he takes great care of them.

They all kneel down to say a few Our Fathers and Hail Marys in chorus; some of the young men try to think about God as they pray, others make no effort to keep their minds away from secular affairs. The Middle Ages

11

valued formal public prayer perhaps more than we do. The act of saying the right words was held to be more important than the right direction of private thoughts.

Now it is time to dress. In general, all gentlemen wear clothes of the same type. The most important garment is the tunic, reaching nearly to the ankle, with sleeves to the wrist. It is put on over the head, and the neckline is low enough to show the top of the shirt, at least in front. Generally speaking, men wear nothing corresponding to our collars; their throats are bare to the collarbone.

There are no pockets in the tunic. But it is kept in place by a girdle around the waist; from this girdle is slung a purse, which can hold odds and ends as well as money. A dagger and perhaps a bunch of keys hang separately from the girdle. The tunic is slit in front from bottom to waist, for convenience in riding and walking.

The tunic is an outer garment, meant to be seen and therefore made of handsome colored cloth. But tunic and shirt alone are not usually enough for the English climate; a surcoat is worn over them except in very warm weather. On this pleasant August morning Ralph and Roger put on sleeveless surcoats with wide holes for arms and neck. The surcoat is slit in front, like the tunic, but its skirts are a few inches shorter to show the handsome garment underneath.

On their legs the boys wear hose, which are long tight stockings. Knitting has not yet been invented, so the hose are made of fine woolen cloth, cut on the bias and shaped to the leg. They fit tightly to well above the knee and then widen so that the drawers may be tucked into them. The well-dressed man takes great care to keep his hose taut and unwrinkled; at the top of them, in front, a tongue of cloth reaches up which is fastened to a "point," a thin cord like a shoestring, coming down from the inner girdle which holds up the drawers. These points must be fastened after the hose are put on. It can be a niggling, awkward job if you are dressing in a hurry, but to appear in public with your points untrussed is very sloppy and disgraceful.

Their shoes are of soft leather, fastened at the ankle with a buckle; the sole is one piece of leather and quite flat. These shoes are expensive luxuries, made carefully to fit; the boys take great care of them and see that they are brushed clean and kept supple with oil.

Probably at some stage of their dressing they will retire to the latrine. This is an odd affair, a little compartment in the outer wall with a wooden seat and a hole going down, like a very small chimney, to the open ground at the foot of the building. From time to time a servant clears away the mess at the bottom. The oddest thing about this little room is its name: it is known as a "garderobe," because in summer fur garments are hung there. The draft blowing constantly through the hole is supposed to keep away moths; and if when winter comes the furs are a bit smelly, they can always be sprinkled with perfume.

Paper is much too rare and expensive to be used in a latrine; instead there are old rags, or wisps of hay.

By this time everyone is dressed, but no one has washed; it is not the custom to carry water up so many stairs from the well in the courtyard. Yet the gentry take great trouble to keep themselves clean; when everyone lives all the time in a crowd it is a part of good manners never to be smelly. The young men go down and crowd around a trough in the yard through which clean water flows. Soap is too expensive to be used every morning, but plenty of water and a scrubbing brush will make hands and faces clean. Everyone has his private towel, hanging on a rail by the washing trough.

After washing, the gentry arrange their hair. The older men wear beards and mustaches, cut short and carefully tended. All have their hair cut, though they leave it longer than we do nowadays. A parting in the middle, with a fringe on the forehead and curls coming down to the nape of the neck at the back, is the style favored by the sons of the Earl and by most other young men.

Combs are carried in the wallet, as big as a modern lady's handbag, which hangs from every gentleman's girdle. In the surcoat is a slit, the ancestor of the modern pocket, which makes it easy to get at the wallet. Mirrors, rare and expensive, are usually of polished metal rather than quicksilver; gentlemen seldom carry them. A peep into a pail of water is enough for a simple hair-brushing.

Now the last touch is added—the little linen cap, known as a coif, that every well-dressed man should wear. It covers the ears and is tied under the chin, but the fringe of hair on the forehead and the curls at the back of the neck are meant to show. Originally the coif was introduced to keep long hair tidy in the open; now it is worn all day, even indoors, and it is always clean and often embroidered. Officially it does not count as a head-covering, and may be worn in church or in the presence of the King.

Correctly dressed, the two boys join the crowd in the castle chapel for morning Mass. Their clothes are alike: red shoes, dark blue hose and surcoat, red tunic, white shirt and coif. Red and dark blue are the Earl's colors, and most of the company wear them.

The sun has just risen as Mass begins. They have all the day before them.

Anne got up a little earlier than her brothers, for she also must be in time for Mass and it takes her longer to dress. Like her brothers, she sleeps in a populous dormitory, surrounded by the ladies who wait on the Countess. Most of these ladies are young unmarried girls, daughters of the Earl's knightly tenants or of his poorer cousins. The ladies run errands for the Countess and help her with her sewing, but they have really come to the household to learn the ways of polite society. It is a form of "coming out," except that they are not looking for husbands; the men they will marry have already been chosen by their parents. By the time they leave the Countess to manage homes of their own they will have learned how to keep house as a lady should.

Young ladies, and the pages who may be their brothers, are often set to perform tasks which we would think more appropriate to hired servants. But a page told to hand around food like a waiter, or a young lady told to help her mistress change her shoes, will never protest that these tasks are beneath their dignity. In the Middle Ages any work, however menial, was considered dignified provided it was done for a social superior. To hold the basin when the King of England was overcome by seasickness was the privilege of a particular noble family and they took pride in it. Any young lady will be glad to hold the towel while the Countess washes her hands, or to comb her hair for her.

The young ladies and the pages get free board and lodging. In theory they get wages also; but these wages are very small, hardly more than pocket money and a gift of clothes at Christmas.

The young ladies do not have their room, known as the bower, all to themselves. They are under the supervision of an elderly widow, a cousin of the Earl's who has no home of her own. In medieval communities there were always a number of these poor and homeless widows, for besides the casualties of constant warfare women tended on the whole to live longer than men. Their kin had to provide for them, and often they found it a problem. There were no country cottages or town apartments where old ladies could live by themselves, and to put them as boarders in a convent was expensive. Madam Eleanor is very grateful to the Countess, but she feels herself to be unwanted and in the way, which makes her short-tempered. In the thirteenth century people who lived too long were not very happy; but finding a proper place for the old is a difficult problem which we still have not solved at the present day.

Since Anne is twelve years old and therefore out of the nursery, she must live with the grownups; there is no halfway house, nothing like our boarding schools. She dresses as a grownup and follows the grown-up routine; but then some pastimes of grown-up life in the Middle Ages were rather childish.

Now she is beginning to dress, helped by several young ladies. The others have gone off to help the Countess, who while her husband is away sleeps almost alone in the state bedchamber; almost alone, because a servant girl sleeps beside her in a little trundle bed which in the daytime is pushed under the state bed. She is there in case the Countess should want anything during the night, for there are no bells in the castle.

Like her brothers, Anne has slept naked. Now she puts on over her head a smock of fine linen, long-skirted and long-sleeved, though neither are long enough to show when she is fully dressed. Then she puts on over her head a kirtle, a long gown with a train. It covers her shoulders but not her neck; its sleeves are made all in one piece with the bodice, very wide under the arms and tapering to the wrist where a lace straps them tight. A plain narrow girdle helps her to adjust the length of her skirt. She wears cloth stockings, kept up by garters tied above the knee, and shoes of the same pattern as a man's, except that they are smaller.

She is now completely dressed, at least for staying indoors in warm weather. Her only underclothing is the smock; if she should tumble downstairs, or fall off her horse, her naked bottom will be displayed—a subject for medieval humor as hackneyed as mother-in-law stories are to us.

Servants bring bowls of water to the bower, so that the

17

ladies may wash and dress their hair before being seen in public. Anne's hair is easily arranged; as a young unmarried girl she wears it parted in the middle and flowing down her back, kept in place by a metal circlet around her head. For great occasions she has a gold circlet, but on this ordinary morning she wears one of engraved bronze.

The other ladies dress their hair in many different ways, unlike the gentlemen, who have fundamentally only one hairstyle. Madam Eleanor, the elderly widow, wears a wimple, a white linen cloth passing under the chin with the lower edge lying loose on her kirtle; on each side it is pinned to the hair above her ears. A kerchief is draped over her head, in front resting on her brow but at the sides and back coming down to her shoulders. Thus her gray hair and withered throat are hidden, and only her face peeps out as though from a hood. It is a fashion kindly to the elderly.

The younger ladies bunch up their hair, either in a net at the back or in two nets over the ears. Instead of a metal circlet they wear a linen band called a fillet, with a separate broader linen band, the barbette, passed tightly from ear to ear under the chin. Thus their faces also seem to peer out from a frame, which is always fetching; yet they display their hair and their smooth young throats, which would be hidden under the wimple which suits old ladies.

This style of hairdressing can be varied in countless ways. The fillet may be so tall that it looks like a saucy little pillbox cap; or its upper edge may be scalloped in imitation of a coronet. On formal occasions the Countess wears a genuine coronet of gold set with gems, but still kept in place by the linen barbette which is kind to sagging jaws. The nets holding her braided hair may be of silk thread or gold wire. Hairdressing is important, and gives plenty of scope to individual fancy.

Everyone in the castle hears Mass every day, which does not mean that they are particularly devout. A king or a great lord may hear three Masses every day without gaining a reputation for exceptional piety: it is the custom. A full High Mass in a great abbey or cathedral takes a long time, though there is splendid singing and gorgeous ritual; but even in a High Mass the Consecration is soon over, and that is the only time a pious layman is expected to fix his thoughts on God. A hundred years earlier King Henry II read letters and dictated the answers during the singing of High Mass, and no one thought the worse of him for it.

This Mass in a private chapel is muttered in less than half an hour. The congregation are there chiefly because it is a convenient place to meet in the morning to discuss the program for the day.

Remember that this short Mass in a private chapel does not fulfill the obligation of hearing Mass *in public* on a Sunday or a great festival. On such a day the Earl and his household ought to attend the parish church, unless they prefer to visit some abbey or cathedral where the service will be more splendid.

After Mass the congregation stand about chatting in the

courtyard. So far no one has had anything to eat, and soon they drift off to the buttery to collect a snack.

We read in early chronicles accounts of huge feasts and get the impression that our ancestors ate a great deal. It would be more accurate to say that they had a few large meals at very long intervals. They might be surprised at our three square meals a day, often with midnight snacks and afternoon tea in addition. The Earl's household expect to eat their fill at dinner, once a day; they have a light supper, though with plenty to drink; breakfast hardly counts as food.

Since the morning is fine the young ladies go off to the flower garden outside the walls, where servants bring them white bread and watered wine. The flower garden is important in the household economy. Water for washing is often scented, and the scent is made at home in the castle stillroom; flowers are used as flavoring in cookery, and garlands are frequently worn. It is the duty of the young ladies to pick flowers by the pound; a pleasant duty, for this is the time when pages and young household knights gather in the garden to pay court to them. But this important side of the education of a young lady will be treated later.

White bread made from wheat is a luxury, eaten daily only by the gentry. It is often flavored with honey or nuts or spices, and baked into buns or fancy rolls. We must not think of Anne and her companions as chewing on stodgy loaves. They drink watered wine because strong wine would make them tipsy, and they have no teetotal drinks. There is no tea, coffee, or cocoa; plain water is not very pleasant on an empty stomach, and anyway it is known to be dangerous to health. It is surprising what strange objects can get into a castle well, and no one has yet thought of boiling water to kill the germs. If anyone made a habit of drinking plain water, and survived, his conduct would be considered so odd that he would get a nickname from it—as witness the many Drinkwaters and Boileaus about at the present day.

Ralph and Roger think it more manly to stand by the buttery door, each with a hunk of rye bread in one hand and a horn of small beer in the other. Their breakfast, eaten standing, takes them only a few minutes.

The sun has not been up an hour, but it is time to begin the work of the day. The boys go off to the stable, where they see the horses groomed and fed. This is a pleasant occupation, but it is work all the same. One day they will be responsible for their own horses, in the field as well as in weathertight stables. There is no better way of learning how to look after horses than watching a competent head groom at work.

When morning stables are finished the boys separate. Roger goes off for lessons with the chaplain; but Ralph can read easily and write after a fashion, which he considers enough book-learning for a future earl. He gets on a quiet elderly destrier to practice riding at the quintain, or tilting post.

For this he does not wear mail. He is still too young for real warfare, and he is growing so fast that it would be foolish to make expensive mail to fit him. But he carries a shield on his left arm, and a close helm on his head, so that his practice will have some of the handicaps of the real thing. His shield is small, triangular, and not too cumbrous. During the last hundred years shields have been growing smaller, as improved mail gives better protection to the legs; there is no need for him to carry a shield which covers him from neck to ankle, as did his ancestor who fought at Hastings. All the same, the shield hampers his left forearm as he holds the reins, and he must get used to riding easily with it.

There are high peaks on his saddle before and behind, to protect a rider whose mail shirt divides at the waist; these make mounting a difficult feat, to be learned by constant practice. The horse's bit is a savage curb set very high in the mouth; a nervous tug at the reins would bring the destrier over backward on his rider. He must ride in correct knightly fashion, legs straight and pointed well forward, toe down, his behind jammed against the back of the saddle so that a blow on his shield will not shift him. To ride like a knight is not easy, but Ralph began practicing seven years ago and he is getting on well.

The close helm still bothers him. It is a heavy pot which covers his whole head and comes down as far as the shoulders. In fact it appears to rest on the shoulders, though a framework within fits over the crown of his head and takes the weight. There is a narrow horizontal slit for him to see through, and lower down a cluster of small holes for breathing. Inside the helm he feels very safe, but he can see only straight ahead and he cannot scratch his nose or brush the sweat out of his eyes. No wonder that most veteran warriors prefer for real battle a steel cap above a neck-covering of chain mail. But the close helm is always worn for tournaments, where opponents often aim at the face. Besides, the summit of a close helm is the only place where Ralph may wear his crest of boiled leather which rises from a wreath of colored silk. Dignity demands that he should know how to ride wearing his crest.

While Ralph rides again and again at a tall pole stuck in the ground Roger is sitting in the chaplain's little room reading aloud from a chronicle written in Latin. He understands what he reads, for the sentences are simply constructed and he knows the meaning of a great many Latin words. If he tries to write his own Latin prose he gets muddled in the grammar. But that is not important, for no layman writes formal letters with his own hand. His father, who sends a good many formal letters, always dictates in French to a clerk; though afterward he looks through the Latin text to make sure that it means what he said.

All the children can speak several languages, because they hear several languages spoken around them. Their mother tongue is Anglo-French, already so different from the French of France that if they should speak it in Paris they would be spotted as foreigners. Roger can write it, and he need not bother about his spelling because Anglo-French has no fixed spelling. But there is only one right way of spelling Latin, which is one reason why laymen avoid writing it. Roger can also speak the English of London, which most merchants anywhere in England can understand. But the peasants on his father's Yorkshire estate speak a different dialect, and in Sussex they speak yet a third. The grooms and servants of the household speak a jargon with as many French words in it as English. That is why no gentleman bothers to learn English correctly; there is no correct way to speak it.

No one writes in English, except a few priests who jot down their sermons so as to be able to use them again. Spelling varies as widely as pronunciation, so that a Dorset parson could hardly understand a sermon written for Northumbrians. The old written Anglo-Saxon that was a learned tongue from the time of King Alfred to the time of Edward the Confessor has become a dead language that no one understands.

Here on the Welsh March the peasants speak yet another language. Neither English nor French is any help in understanding it, and the only thing to do is to learn a few phrases by heart. If Roger got lost in the hills he could ask the way home in Welsh, and understand the answer. But when a Welsh minstrel performs in the hall Roger just listens to the pleasant music.

No one despises the Welsh, for they are not a subject race. They have their own nobility; if Prince Llewellyn was good enough to marry a daughter of King John, then other princes are good enough to marry the daughters of Marcher lords. The Earl has a number of Welsh cousins; but of course, like the gentry in any other part of Christendom, these Welsh gentry can speak French.

During his lessons Roger has acquired a picture of the world he lives in. He knows that it is round; he has only to look at the sea to know that, though some ignorant inland peasants think differently. But more than half of the round world whose shadow causes eclipses of the moon (he knows that also) is inaccessible to the human race. On the equator lies a belt of heat that would fry any explorer who tried to cross it. South of the equator is presumably another temperate zone very like this, but with no men in it. There cannot be any, for a conclusive theological reason. Our Lord died to bring the chance of salvation to all mankind; but if no man can cross the equator the Gospel cannot be preached in the Southern Hemisphere. Therefore in the Southern Hemisphere there are no men with immortal souls.

The inhabited world is a rectangle which can easily be represented on a flat map. It is bounded on the west by the Atlantic, on the north by Arctic ice, on the south by the African desert, on the east—well, no one has been that far, but they say that beyond the limits of the immense Mongol Empire lies another great ocean.

Jerusalem is the center of this land mass. East of Jerusalem dwell Arabs and Turks and Indians, infidels who hardly concern a young nobleman of England. Jerusalem itself matters, of course; every knight should join in the effort to regain it for Christendom. As a young man the Earl went on crusade for a year or two, and the boys expect to make the long journey to Syria one day. But they will not stay very long in the Holy Land, and they scarcely hope for victory. The Crusade has been waged for nearly three hundred years, and it is beginning to be apparent that the infidels are too strong

25

for us. The King now reigning, Edward I, went on crusade as a young man; no subsequent king of England will attempt it.

All Africa is under infidel rule, though many Christians still live in Egypt. There are infidels also in Spain, though they seem to be getting the worst of the Holy War. Not long ago the Kingdom of Portugal was set up after a fleet of English crusaders had liberated Lisbon; if you want to go crusading at a bargain, without the toilsome voyage to Syria, Spain offers an attractive substitute. An even simpler alternative, since little sea travel is involved, is to fight the heathen in Prussia; but then you will have to join an army of Germans, who do not get on well with French-speaking knights.

In any other part of the civilized world, from Hungary to Portugal, from Flanders to Sicily, a knight will find himself among knights of his own kind, gentlemen who follow the same code of manners, who speak French after a fashion even if they use another language by the fireside, whose clerks write letters in exactly the same Latin. Roger likes to hear about foreign countries, for perhaps he will settle in one of them. The plans for his future are still vague, but obviously he cannot stay at home after his brother has succeeded to the earldom.

When his mother dies Roger will come into a small estate, the few manors she brought to her husband when she married him. They may go to a younger son without impairing the strength of the earldom. He might find a bride with a little land of her own, though a great heiress would not be given in marriage to a younger son. He might live quietly in the country on a meager revenue. But he wants to do better than that. He hopes to serve some king or great lord until he is rewarded with a wide estate, and perhaps founds another branch of his famous and noble family.

He will try the King of England first, naturally, because in England his family influence will be most useful to him. But he may not like the King, or the courtiers around him. Then he may go to any other court in Christendom without being reproached for disloyalty. Noblemen are above nationality. To begin with he will serve as an unpaid volunteer, or for a monthly wage; but if he is to get anywhere he will presently have to choose a lord and take oath to him. It may be the King of Hungary, or the Bishop of Liège, or any other potentate who leads an army. He will not be deserting his native land. All Christendom is his native land.

He will serve his lord by fighting for him, of course. That is what he is being trained to do, and it is the normal occupation for one of his birth. But if he is to gain a good reward he will have to be more than a valiant knight. If he is honest about money and capable in administration he may be made governor of some outlying fief. A ruler always needs as many competent and honest subordinates as he can find. A household knight of King Edward I might rise from castellan of a small fortress to commander of a frontier town to governor of a province in France. If Roger tries hard, and is lucky, he may die a greater man than his brother the Earl.

That is why he is now learning history and geography,

to fit himself for a senior post in the royal service. The history he learns is concerned only with great men of the past and their ups and downs, but it will teach him all the political theory current in his world. Geography is half military, half commercial, and teaches him as much on the subject of administration as he can learn from books.

Meanwhile Anne has been going around the castle with the chatelaine, the wife of the castellan who lives there all the year round and commands the garrison in the absence of the Earl. They have inspected the kitchens and the storerooms and the well and the drains, and visited the sick. They found all in order. Everything stinks a bit, but then it is summertime. There are no piles of decaying offal in the kitchen, no maggots in the salt meat, only one dead sparrow in the well and they saw it fished out; none of the drains are completely blocked with filth. A sick groom lies babbling in a high fever, though the chief cook has let blood from his arm; but there are no boils on his skin, and it is to be hoped that his sickness is not infectious.

If plague should strike the castle the Countess would send off her children, and perhaps her husband would command her to go too. But most of the knights and squires would stay to look after the sick; for to flee from plague after it has appeared is considered as disgraceful as to flee from the battlefield, though it is permissible to avoid an epidemic by going to a remote or healthy spot before the infection has struck.

You cannot help the sick except by keeping them warm and fed and clean. There are medicines in plenty, but no one expects them to do any good. Surgery is a more useful art; it can be learned by experience, and with so much fighting going on it is easy to get experience in dressing wounds. Every lady should know how to bandage a wound, and how to set a broken limb. Anne has practiced sewing up an open cut, on the carcass of a pig in the larder; she hopes she will never have to do it in earnest, but a time may come when lives depend on her skill.

Anne is not an important heiress, since she has two healthy brothers. All the same, she is sought after as a wife. Her father will give her a valuable dowry in money and jewels; and her husband will profit by his connection with a powerful family. This husband is not yet chosen, but her parents are busy at the task. Within the next few years, before her sixteenth birthday, she will certainly be married to someone.

Although she is happy at home she looks forward to early marriage, for delay may be dangerous. If the Earl should die while his sons are under age and his daughter unmarried, the King, his overlord, will at once assume all the legal rights of the head of the family, including the right to arrange Anne's marriage. He will not exercise this right with any regard for her happiness. This unpleasant custom was never questioned by men of the Middle Ages, though they were in general merciful to ladies. The King's wards are royal assets, to be exploited to their full monetary value. If an heir is under age the

King takes his whole income, though of course he must see that the boy enjoys board and lodging suitable to his rank. Heiresses are sold in marriage to the highest bidder, or given as rewards to faithful royal servants. Or the marriage of a young heiress may be sold for cash down while she is still a child, the buyer having the right to marry her to the man of his choice when she is old enough. The only check on this practice, acknowledged even by a king, is that he must not disparage a noble lady: that is, marry her to someone who is not her peer in social rank. The husband, provided he is a gentleman, may be very old or very wicked or very disgusting. A wicked king, however, will not stop at disparagement, and may give his wards to men of infamous birth. That is a breach of feudal custom; but the only way to stop him is by a general rebellion of all his barons, who will put up with a good deal before they start a civil war.

So Anne is naturally anxious to be married while her father is still alive. Her parents share her anxiety; and though nothing has yet been settled they are looking around for a suitable match.

Negotiations have been started with two candidates. Sir John is a wealthy baron, nearly as powerful as the Earl, an honorable knight distinguished in the wars, a good man who will treat his wife as he should. But he is in his fifties, a widower with several sons, bad-tempered and crochety because always plagued by rheumatism and gout, mean over money. His will be a dull household, and if his wife does not run it efficiently he might beat her. Barring accidents, he will die before her, and when his son by his first marriage inherits the baronry, she will find herself an unwanted stepmother. Besides, Anne considers him ugly.

On the other hand, widowhood as an unwanted stepmother would have its advantages. Her dowry from her father and the dower provided from her late husband's land would give her enough to live on in modest comfort; and no one would mind if she contracted a second marriage with the man of her choice. In the Middle Ages there were few love matches; but there were some, and they were usually between young widows and gentlemen in the household of the late husband.

Sir James, the other candidate, is a gay young knight only ten years older than Anne herself. He is handsome, and sings and dances very well. But at present he is poor; and though such a knight will go far if he lives, he can make his reputation only by living dangerously. Any day he might be killed in battle, leaving his widow in poverty. His other drawback is a roving eye; he is always desperately in love with some lady, but never for long with the same lady. He might consider a wife a handicap, and keep her shut up in the country while he peacocks about at tournaments and feasts. There is no reason to suppose he will fall in love with Anne; he wants to marry her only because being the son-in-law of an earl will help him in his career. Unless he dies in battle she may expect to be tied to him for life, with no chance of a second marriage of affection.

There is much to be said on either side, and Anne has not yet made up her mind. For, though she must choose between these two candidates, her father leaves her the final choice. As a father he prefers to see his daughter happy, and if he forces her into a marriage which she loathes his friends will think the worse of him. In the Middle Ages fathers were no more unfeeling than they are now; most really distasteful marriages were contracted because the matchmakers in an excess of prudence thought too much about money, rather than because they were indifferent to the happiness of their children.

Anne has a last line of defense, though only a girl of strong character can make use of it. Though no daughter may marry without the consent of her parents, when the time comes for the wedding her own consent will be necessary. If she has the courage to answer No when the officiating priest asks her the vital question, the Church will step in to forbid the match, and even an earl dare not defy the Church. Of course her parents are entitled to persuade her to change her mind, and their persuasion may be very forceful—bread and water, beatings, imprisonment in a little room. But if she can stick it out she will not be married against her will; though probably that means she will never marry at all, never become the mistress of her own household.

That is what most ladies marry for—independence, the freedom of ruling a household. To be mistress of a great castle is obviously more pleasant than to pig it in a poor manor, and therefore many daughters agree with their fathers that the richest and most powerful husband must also be the best. The personality of the bridegroom is less important; he will be away most of the time, anyway.

So Anne is pondering the question of her marriage. She is also thinking about Love. But she keeps Love in a separate compartment of her mind, for it has nothing to do with marriage. Courteous love is the chief occupation of castle-dwellers, one might almost say their favorite hobby.

All the grownups in the castle are in love all the time; and they frequently change the object of their affections. These love affairs are not intended to lead to anything, certainly not to marriage; for one thing, most of the participants are already married. Gentlemen sigh and protest their devotion, and perform exploits in honor of their ladies. A lady may grant some trifle from her dress, a sleeve or a kerchief, to be worn by the knight as proof that he comes first in her affections; or she may show it merely by asking him to play chess or backgammon with her after supper. In all this there will be a strong element of competition. The lady collects as many suitors as she can, perhaps by stealing them from other ladies; many knights would rather be second among the suitors of a popular beauty than first with someone who is considered dowdy and out of fashion.

A knight may prove his devotion by other means than slaying dragons or unhorsing his rivals in a tourney. Flirtation is recognized as a minor art, and skill in this art brings favor and renown. Witty, well-turned compliments are admired; so is good conversation in general; and so especially are tuneful singing and neat verse. A suitor ought to be able to compose a song in honor of his lady, and sing it pleasantly to his own accompaniment; though the accompaniment will be rather a few twangs on a stringed instrument to mark the cadence of the verse than anything we would nowadays call a tune.

A squire and two or three pages of the household have already begun to court the lady Anne. At first it made her feel shy, but now she finds it amusing. Early this morning one of the pages was with her in the flower garden, comparing each of her features in turn to the flowers she was picking. She made quite a neat reply, comparing him to a too anxious gardener who waters plants when they do not need it. The other ladies laughed, and she felt very poised and grown up.

Of course these youths, and the occasional knight who joins them, are faithful followers of the Earl her father. They would never annoy the daughter of their lord, or tease her if she were not in the mood for flirtation. This sharpening of wits is great fun, and will continue until Anne is an old woman. Most of the senior knights profess to be dying for love of her mother.

If some man lost his head and tried to take her in his arms she would call for help and he would be killed at once. An attractive young lady has the best of both worlds, constant courtship without any real danger. The whole affair is a game, a pastime in the most literal sense of the word.

Time is passing, while everyone is busy at some useful work. The ladies have settled down to their embroidery, knights and squires are fussing over horses and weapons, clerks are writing. In the kitchen they are busiest of all.

About the fifth hour a horn is blown, to warn the household to get ready for dinner.

That brings us to the question of time-keeping, which was difficult in a period when there were few clocks. Day and night were divided into twenty-four hours, as now; but twelve o'clock came at sunrise and sunset. So the fifth hour was five hours after sunrise and an hour before midday, though it did not correspond exactly with our 11 A.M. This is August, and there is more daylight than dark; therefore each of the twelve hours of day will be longer than an hour of night. What the chief cook does, of course, is to glance at the sun and decide that it is five-sixths of its way from the horizon to its highest point. Monks, who must pray in choir every three hours throughout the day, pay more attention to time. In some monasteries there are genuine mechanical clocks, and in others an arrangement of water dripping slowly through a small hole. But in secular life no one bothers about a few minutes either way.

Ralph hands over his tired horse to a groom; Roger runs downstairs to the courtyard, leaving his teacher to put away the pens and books of the last lesson; Anne sorts into their boxes the colored threads of her embroidery. All the men and boys are soon gathered around the washing trough, borrowing combs from one another and peeping at their faces in any standing water they can find. The Earl's sons run upstairs to put on finer surcoats and shoes than they have worn in the morning.

Servants carry bowls of scented water to the bower, where all the ladies are bringing out their mirrors.

Dinner is not only the chief meal of the day, it is a considerable ceremony. The hall, the largest room in the castle, soon fills with waiting hungry figures. Servants have placed three trestle tables lengthways down it, with benches on both sides; on the dais, the platform at the upper end, a shorter table is set at right angles. This is covered with a fine linen cloth, and the seats are on one side only, facing the body of the hall. There are two carved armchairs in the middle, and the other seats are plainer but individual chairs or stools.

Midway down each of the long tables is a saltcellar, an elaborate and fanciful piece of silver plate. As we all know (perhaps the only thing we all know about medieval etiquette), the gentry sit on the dais side of this salt, and the common people at the same table below it.

The knights and ladies of the household stand by their places; upper servants are standing close beside them. Of course a number of people cannot eat at this time, because they are needed to prepare or serve the meal. The cooks eat in the kitchen, before or after the others; in addition the pages, some of the younger squires, and a number of servingmen are waiting to carve or pass the dishes. They are supposed to eat later.

The tables have been laid, though to our eyes they look bare. At each place is a horn or wooden spoon, perhaps a leather or horn drinking mug, and a substantial hunk of bread. No other eating implements are provided, for each diner will bring his own. At the last minute an under-butler arranges before each place at the high table a little ornamental box, containing the private napkin, knife, and spoons of the distinguished person who will sit there. The napkin is of very fine linen, and the other things mostly pure silver; table equipment of this kind is a recognized field for display. The individual boxes are usually shaped like a toy ship; so that "nef," French for ship, is the common name for them.

At last the Countess and her party emerge onto the dais from the solar, the little private room at the upper end of the hall. At the same time a procession of butlers and servingmen enter from the lower door which leads to the kitchen. Ralph and Anne are among the party at the high table; but Roger, who is still a page, stands with his fellows by one of the carving tables.

A clerk says grace, and as the company sit down butlers climb the dais carrying the dishes of the first course. That word "course" is rather a puzzle where it occurs in descriptions of medieval meals; for there was no regular sequence of dishes, from soup to dessert, as we have nowadays. This first course comprises every kind of sweet and savory dish, which may be eaten in any order. Nevertheless, there will be three courses in all, each containing all these various things. The most likely explanation is that a course was made up of as many dishes as could be cooked at once, and that in the kitchen they are now busy dishing up the second course.

For the upper classes, for all who live in castles, roast meat is the staff of life. They eat a good deal of flour as well, baked in various ways; but they hardly notice that.

Vegetables seldom appear on the table. There are of course no potatoes; other roots, carrot and onion, are served only as flavoring in stews; cabbage is despised as the food of the poor. Salads of lettuce and other greens, and fresh fruit, are avoided by the timid as dangerous to health. So they will be, of course, if they come in from the garden dirty and no one remembers to wash them.

At this dinner the main dish is roast beef. An ox, specially fattened, is killed to feed the castle every morning. But one ox is not enough for the large company in the hall, so there are also pork and mutton. All the animals have just been killed. There is no idea of hanging meat for a few days to make it tender.

For fresh meat is a seasonal luxury, and soon the season will be over. At Michaelmas, the 29th of September, there will be a great slaughter of cattle, leaving alive only the breeding stock and the indispensable plow oxen. There are no rutabagas or turnips, no winter fodder except hay; it is impossible to keep many beasts alive after the grass has stopped growing. From autumn until spring everyone will have to make do with salt beef and salt pork from the Michaelmas slaughtering; except that at the high table they will sometimes have venison, which can be killed all the year round since no one bothers about a close season for hunting.

That is one reason why the right to hunt is so highly valued. On his Welsh land the Earl may hunt deer, but in England only hares and rabbits. All English deer, no matter who holds the woodlands, are reserved for the King, so that at court they may eat fresh venison all through the winter. If the King is in a good temper he may grant the Earl permission to take a few deer in his own woods; otherwise even a noble family will have to live on salt meat, badly cured and smelly, a challenge to the skill of the best cooks.

After the roast meats of the first course have been displayed to the Countess they are carried to the carving tables at the side of the hall. Carving is an art which every squire must master, and the pages are learning it; Roger must do his best to cut a piece of beef into neat collops. He has a sharp carving knife, but no fork; and it is very bad manners to touch the meat except with the first two fingers of the left hand. He finds his task difficult.

During the carving servants give out plates. At the lower tables these are made of beechwood, which is close-grained and may be scrubbed clean. At the high table they have manchets, big round slices of wheaten bread thick enough to soak up the gravy. If you are feeling hungry you may afterward eat your gravy-soaked manchet, but it is better manners to leave it for the beggars at the castle gate.

Everyone has his own plate; but the meat, after it has been carved, is placed in dishes between each couple. Ladies and gentlemen sit alternately, and the lady who shares a gentleman's dish is his partner throughout dinner, whom he should entertain with conversation. By this time the beef has grown cold, but nobody bothered about eating food hot until quite late in the eighteenth century.

Ralph's table manners are excellent. The silver-hilted

knife he takes out of his nef is very clean, and so are his hands. With the two courtesy fingers of his left hand he steadies the lump of beef in the dish while he cuts small pieces from it and transfers them on the point of his knife to the manchet of the lady sitting beside him. He tries to make each piece small enough to be a single mouthful, so that the lady will not have to use her own knife. When she has been fed he can begin to eat. The lady uses a spoon, to keep her hands clean.

Meanwhile butlers have been serving drink: French wine for the high table and strong ale for the others. At the lower tables everyone has his own mug, of horn or leather, which he brings into the hall with him; but at the high table there is a great silver cup for each couple. This means that every lady or gentleman must eat carefully, and use a napkin. It is very bad manners to leave on the rim of the cup any evidence that you have drunk from it.

Ralph and his partner, both young and vigorous, choose beef as their main dish in the first course. But Anne is paired with an elderly knight, the constable of the castle, and out of kindness to him she has asked for her dish to be filled with a savory stew. The teeth of the old constable cannot cope with a solid roast. In those days there were men who made a living by pulling out aching teeth, but they were considered such scoundrels that "tooth-drawer" was a standard term of abuse. There was no other form of dentistry, and of course no false teeth. Elderly people held on to their teeth as long as they could, even if the teeth were too tender to be used;

if a bad tooth was pulled out it would leave an unsightly gap. Constant pain from unsound teeth was one of the normal penalties of age. That is why in this dinner there are as many stews and minces and thick soups as solid dishes.

As a centerpiece on the high table the chief cook has made a "subtlety," a tower of pastry complete with battlements and arrow-slits; it is garnished with nuts and almond paste, and on top is a little watchman made of sugar. The inside is flavored with honey and sweet raisins. But today the Countess does not cut into it, and no one else wishes to be the first to spoil the design; at the end of dinner it is removed intact to decorate the table on another day.

There are many sweet dishes, made chiefly of honey, cream, and fruit. There are also some remarkable mixtures, like the mince pies we eat at Christmas, in which meat of strong flavor is mingled with spices and honey and pepper until you cannot tell whether they are meant to taste sweet or savory. The very strong flavor appeals to elderly people afflicted with chronic catarrh, who cannot appreciate anything more delicate. On this ordinary day no sugar appears on the table except for the untouched subtlety. Sugar is an expensive luxury, imported at great cost from Spain or the infidel lands beyond Jerusalem. The normal sweetening is honey from local hives.

Everyone eats what pleases him best: roast meat for the young and hungry, soups and stews for those with tender teeth, mixed flavors for those who can hardly

41

taste anything. Presently the second course is brought in, composed of much the same dishes as the first.

When the third and last course has been carved the pages may begin their dinner. Roger goes to the seat kept for him at a side table, where the other pages struggle for places. They devour the remains of the first course, now cold and rather messy; but to live on leftovers is part of the training of a page, and they do not grumble.

At length everyone has eaten enough to last him until the next square meal, that is to say until dinner tomorrow. The Countess rises and brings the meal to an end before anyone can drink too much. It is not long after midday, but in one sense the day is finished. All the gentry feel that they have done a good day's work, which we must remember began at dawn; the remaining hours of daylight may be devoted to amusement.

Though the evenings are drawing in, summer routine continues until Michaelmas. Most people go to their bedrooms for a nap; or they find a quiet corner somewhere and play chess or backgammon with friends. What you may not do, in a well-run castle, is loaf in the hall until suppertime with a drink before you. That would encourage drunkenness, so the servants have strict orders to remove the benches as soon as dinner is finished.

The Countess and her steward retire to the little room at the back of the hall, the solar, where they may be private. There are money matters to be discussed, and since they concern young Ralph he is summoned to attend. It is about time he had a destrier of his own, and the question to be decided is whether the family can afford it.

The castle appears to be run regardless of expense, but the steward pays out very little silver for housekeeping. All the mass of food consumed every day comes from the Earl's land, and the numerous servants get little more than their keep and a present at Christmas. So long as the Earl keeps hold of his estates he can live in this way without worrying about money. But a destrier must be bought, for coined silver. Any expenditure from the hoard in the strongbox calls for careful thought.

The trouble is, as it was with every great household in the Middle Ages, that there is no way of foretelling next year's income. Beef and grain come from the land. So does wool, which is made up into everyday clothing by weavers in the nearest town. But hardly any annual rents are paid in silver.

The big strongbox in the main tower contains a quantity of silver, chiefly the pennies which have been struck by all the kings of England since Canute with little alteration in their weight or fineness. No other English coins exist, though clerks keep their accounts in pounds and shillings because the custom has come down from the days of the later Roman Empire. Weight of metal is what matters, not the design on the coin; a clipped penny is worth less than a whole one. Foreign coins pass current as easily as English, and so do halfpennies and farthings made by cutting the silver penny along the lines of the large cross which fills one face of it. Most of the foreign coins in the hoard are French, very small and debased. In France the great nobles strike their own coins, and have made such a mess of it that now many mints issue *solidi*, shillings worth nominally twelve pennies, which are no larger than English pence. In French they are called *sous*, but you must add where they came from. The sou of Tours is not necessarily of the same value as the sou of Champagne.

In a separate compartment are a few pieces of gold: bezants from Constantinople, florins from Tuscany, queer coins from Moslem Spain or Africa with lettering on them that no Christian can read. These are regarded rather as metal than as current coin. Once the late King Henry III issued a gold penny in imitation of the Tuscan florin. It was soon withdrawn, at the petition of the London merchants. They complained that such a valuable piece of money was no use to them, since one gold penny was worth more than the whole contents of the average London shop; in fact they disliked it because gold is not reckoned as money, and fluctuates in price like any other commodity.

The Earl regards his gold as a handy raw material for coronets and brooches, or as a suitable gift to offer at a shrine. He would never attempt to pay a bill with it, for that would entail long haggling over its value.

The Earl's money comes in irregularly, in windfalls; so it is impossible to budget prudently for the future. The ransom of a knight taken in war is always a good sum, but the present border skirmishes do not bring in the plentiful ransoms of the old French war. Otherwise his main source of ready cash is the death of a knightly tenant, an event which cannot be calculated in advance. When an heir takes over the estate of his dead father he must pay his overlord a relief, a sum reckoned at about a year's income of the fief. If the dead knight's heir is under age, or if he leaves a marriageable widow with land of her own, there will be the valuable rights of wardship, explained previously. Serfs may want to buy their freedom, though the lord must be careful not to leave his manor shorthanded in the future for the sake of cash in hand. Perhaps a growing village will want to buy the charter that will make it a town, or the right to hold a weekly market. But there are already a great number of chartered towns and weekly markets in the earldom, and vested interests must be preserved; that source of income was pretty well exhausted fifty years ago by the Earl's father.

On some manors every household pays an annual hearth penny; on others nothing is paid in cash. Surplus cattle and corn can be sold in the market, but until the harvest has been gathered no one knows whether there will be a surplus. The wisest steward cannot foretell his lord's income in money for next year.

On the Continent a nobleman may tax his peasants whenever he finds himself short of money. In England this right to exact a tallage from serfs and an aid from free tenants is closely restricted by law. The Earl will levy a tax on his tenants to pay for the festivities when Ralph is knighted, and again for Anne's wedding. Except for his own ransom if he should happen to be captured in battle, that finishes the list. He must pay out of his own hoard for Roger's knighting; the tax may be levied only for the eldest son and the eldest daughter.

From his hoard the Earl pays the household wages at

Christmas, probably his heaviest regular expenditure in money. Other expenditures may come when least expected. He must keep in with the King; the law is so complicated, the right to any great fief so tangled, that a concerted attack by the King's judges can ruin any great landholder. Luckily, even if you annoy the King you may buy his good will for cash down. This is a regular commercial transaction, which will be entered bluntly in the royal accounts: So-and-so has paid so much to have the King's friendship and benevolence. King Edward honestly keeps his side of the bargain; unlike his grandfather John, who would sell his benevolence every three months and still remain as malevolent as ever.

But the King may be hard pressed financially, and then he will demand a subsidy from the great lords. These lords must give their consent, of course; but if the money is needed for the defense of the realm they will grant it. Then, within a very short time, each lord must pay over his share.

The time will come, inevitably, when the King will demand a great sum from the fief: when the Earl is dead and Ralph is due to inherit. Magna Carta fixed the relief for an ordinary baronial fief at the reasonable rate of a year's income; but earldoms were omitted from this arrangement. The King takes as much as he can get; the only limit to his rapacity is that the other earls may take fright and revolt if he asks too much.

For all these unforeseeable emergencies—to pay his ransom if he is captured, to pay an unexpected tax, to pay the relief when he dies—the Earl must keep a great sum of money always by him. He cannot keep it in the bank, since there are no banks. He will find it very hard to borrow for a sudden emergency. No Christian may lend money at usury, and the Jews who used to do so have been ruined by royal exactions. If the Earl is in real trouble he might pawn a piece of land; the lender will take the harvest, and for some reason that does not count as usury. But that is a very desperate course. If a man is so hard pressed that he must pawn land it is unlikely that he will ever be rich enough to get it back; the fief will be permanently diminished.

All great lords need a hoard of money to make them feel safe. Since they all keep their silver shut up, the ordinary commercial world is always short of ready cash. Throughout the Middle Ages no one liked to part with silver; though in a great emergency, to ransom a king or hire mercenaries to avert an invasion, huge sums could be produced.

In the end Ralph gets his destrier, for the heir to a great earldom must be properly mounted. The steward trusts to luck that more money will come in soon; perhaps a rich vassal will die so that his heir pays a good relief. But Ralph must be careful in other ways, and so must the other children. While they are in the country, on their father's land, they need spend no money at all, except to give an occasional penny to a beggar or a shrine.

After an hour's rest Anne and Roger meet Ralph in the courtyard. Their duties are finished for the day, and they may amuse themselves together. What they would like better than anything else would be to get out the hounds and look for a stag. But the right to hunt was granted to the Earl, and there may be complaints if the family go hunting in his absence, complaints from neighbors or from the King's powerful foresters. Besides, the great event of hunting a stag should occupy the whole day, and now the afternoon is drawing on. As the next best thing, they decide to go hawking.

Ralph has a peregrine of his own, which he is training himself. He carries her about with him whenever he gets the chance, so that she will know him and get used to crowds of other people. The best way to get her accustomed to crowds is to take her to church, perched on his wrist. From time to time he does this, but not so often as he would like. Sooner or later the clergy complain to his father. Hawks in church are a standing cause of quarrels between clerks and laity. Falconers point out that the hooded birds sit quietly and cause no disturbance; clerks reply that the brute creation must be kept out of church, even if it behaves quietly.

Ralph's hawk, her eyes covered by her hood, will always stay quiet on his wrist. When he removes the hood and throws her into the air she will chase her quarry. Then comes the critical moment: will she return when her master waves his lure? Sometimes she does and sometimes she doesn't. But even the best hawks do not always answer the lure, and Ralph is satisfied with her.

Anne has a little goshawk; though it is looked after by the falconer in the mews and she sees it only when she goes hawking. She is rather frightened of its sharp beak, and seldom takes off the hood. In fact she is not fond of hawking as a pastime. But a hawk on the wrist looks decorative, and is in addition a mark of gentle birth.

Roger, who is still learning falconry, has no hawk of his own. In the mews he practices hooding and unhooding, which need deft fingers and a sure touch. He has watched the head falconer "seal" a new-taken bird, sewing together her eyelids to make her dependent on her captors and obedient to them. But he has not yet been trusted to try it himself, for a slip with the needle might damage her eyes. Hawks can be a danger to the unskillful, and a young man with a finger missing will be handicapped in the handling of his weapons. But the chief reason why hawks are treated with great care is that they are very expensive; the best come from far-off Iceland, and there are never very many of them on the market. You will note, by the way, that the best hawks were hens; nowadays a great many people forget that.

The children are mounted on light handy ponies. Hawking is a sport best practiced on horseback. But there is a great deal of standing about, varied with short gallops over rough ground; a mettlesome destrier would be a nuisance, and a sober hackney not fast enough.

The chief falconer comes with them, to keep an eye on the valuable birds. This falconer came up from the ranks; in the hall he sits below the salt, though only just below it. Even so, he is a considerable personage and the children obey his instructions. On some fiefs the chief falconer is of gentle birth; it is one of the few crafts which a

49

gentleman may follow without loss of dignity. The Emperor Frederick II, the mightiest ruler of the last generation, wrote an immense treatise on falconry; the hobby of an emperor must be socially correct.

The chief falconer brings a crowd of grooms and austringers, the men on foot who carry little square frames on which the hawks can sit. The children of an earl should not go out without an escort, and in the castle there are always plenty of spare hands. Nobody at that time tried to save labor, since there was more of it than could be used. The more men the Earl employs the greater he will be. They expect no more than board and lodging and a present at Christmas, for in a castle they may sleep safe.

The children ride to a bushy valley through which flows a little stream. Beaters and spaniels plunge through the bushes to flush any birds that may be there. Coots are quarry enough for Anne's goshawk, and the beaters put up a mallard who is worthy of the peregrine. Meanwhile the children ride their ponies a little way up the slope, and cast off their hawks when the falconer advises. There is no sport if you loose your hawk when the quarry is too close, but your bird may fly away forever if you give her too many long stern chases. In this, as in every other branch of falconry, there are many books of instruction; but the only way to learn well is by practice under the direction of a master.

The peregrine towers above her quarry, then drops on it like a stone. That is thrilling to watch, but you can see it from a long way off; you then ride to the kill to lure her back to your wrist. The pursuit of the goshawk, though not so spectacular, is really more fun if you are well mounted. She chases her quarry from behind, following every dodge and turn. You must ride hard to keep her in view, and be up at the kill if you are to lure her success-fully. Secretly Roger thinks that goshawks are more fun than peregrines; it is a pity that they are suitable to be carried only by ladies and clerks.

Ralph gets a brace of eatable duck, and Anne collects several useless trophies. But the bag is not important. A hawk ought always to catch her quarry if she is properly cast off; what matters is that she should sit quietly until needed, come back willingly to the lure, and consent to be hooded without resistance. The children are learning how to train their hawks in these things.

Listening to the chief falconer they are also learning the language of falconry. Almost every action of the bird has a name of its own, a name that would never be used for the same action by a beast or a man. It is an intricate and rather silly branch of learning, but every lady or gentleman must know it perfectly; a self-made man, a bishop of humble birth or a successful captain of merce-naries, will always give himself away if he talks about falconry.

The children cover several miles of the valley, and then turn for home in time to be back by sunset. They are riding over their father's land, where the crops are nearly ripe for harvest. They have a right to ride where they please, through standing grain if need be; but to trample growing crops would be to harm the peasants who look to them for protection and to diminish their father's revenue. They try to remember to go around by the headlands, unless they are very excited. Peasants are always complaining that the gentry trample their crops; the gentry maintain that this happens rarely, unless hounds are running hard or a hawk has killed in the middle of a field. It is considered bad manners to do unnecessary damage. But the gentry are the judges of whether the damage was necessary or not.

The children do not think of hawking as lessons, but all the time they have been learning their duties. One day they will be responsible for wide estates. They must be able to recognize good plowing, good manuring, good sowing, to see whether a barn is well built or a gate well hung. Any improvement on the land must be inspired by the lord at the top; peasants never do anything that was not done by their fathers before them.

After their scamper over the fields they are scratched and tousled and sweating. On the way home the boys drop behind, strip, and have a quick bath in the stream. The water is too cold to be pleasant, though they pretend to enjoy it; but young squires who wish to please the ladies must frequently wash themselves all over, and this is as good a way as any of doing it. Anne cannot bathe in the open. She is just as hot and dirty as her brothers, but she must wait until she gets home and then do her best with a bowl of warm water in the bower. The other ladies will help her, and she also will be clean in the evening.

Once a month the children have a genuine hot bath, with soap and towels. It cannot be done more often, for it makes a great deal of extra work in the kitchen. The tall wooden tub must be placed in some quiet corner of the courtyard; water must be heated in big metal cauldrons; many servants are needed to carry it from the kitchen to the bath; someone in authority must take out the towels and soap from the locked store-cupboard. As a rule the children bathe after the Countess, and after the Earl if he is at home. Frequently more hot water is added to the tub, but it is not completely emptied until everyone has finished with it. A hot bath is a pleasure, as greatly appreciated in the thirteenth century as in the twentieth; but if your only source of hot water is a cauldron hanging over a wood fire you cannot bathe every day.

A steam bath is an even rarer luxury, because it needs skilled preparation. Everyone remembers that the ancient Romans wallowed in these wonderful baths, which were denounced by some early Christian Fathers as a sinful indulgence. An aura of wickedness and dissipation still hangs over the hot baths of Aix, where some of the Roman routine continued throughout the Dark Ages. In Italy also there are steam baths, and returned crusaders tell of those they have seen in the East. But steam baths must be built by an expert, unless you are lucky enough to have a natural hot spring by your door. The steam is produced by heating large stones in the kitchen, carrying them with tongs to the little bathing cabin, then pouring water over them. If you do this without expert guidance you will probably set your house or castle on fire. Sixty years ago King John had a full-time bathman, whose sole work was to prepare the steam bath wherever the King might be stopping.

Since there is no bathman in this castle there are no steam baths. Occasionally the Countess has one if she happens to be at court or in some other place where they are available. It is one of the treats the children look forward to when they are grown up.

Yet all the gentry keep themselves very clean, unless they are actually on the battlefield. It is one of the distinctions which mark them off from the often smelly lower classes. They have plenty of cold water and plenty of clean clothes; with these advantages you need never be dirty, even though there is no bathtub within reach. Ask any old soldier, and remember that every castle was full of old soldiers.

By suppertime, which is soon after sunset, everyone is neat and clean; those who have taken exercise during the afternoon have changed their clothes. The boys have put on embroidered sleeveless surcoats and thin hose of fine colored cloth; of course they wear clean linen shirts and clean coifs. Anne wears a kirtle with a long train; her hair still flows down her back, but the circlet which keeps it in place is of silver gilt.

Supper is not so formal as dinner. Most of the gentry take their places in the hall, but many of those who would sit below the salt collect food from the kitchen and take it to their own quarters. Most of the food is cold, the remains of what was cooked for dinner. But there is plenty of wine, or beer at the lower tables, and a general air of leisure and recreation; people eat slowly, since when they leave the hall there will be nothing to do but go to bed.

As the day fades torches are lit in the wall sconces; these are mostly of pine wood, giving plentiful light amid a shower of sparks. A few candles stand on the high table, two of best beeswax beside the Countess and others of smelly tallow toward the ends. Wax candles are costly, and carefully guarded. Every evening fresh candles are lit on the high table, in keeping with the Earl's dignity; but the leftovers are valuable perquisites, and everyone knows where they should go—the beeswax candle ends to the clerks; those of tallow to stewards, huntsmen, falconers—in general, to anyone who will have to write or make out lists in the evening. On the stairs of the castle a few rush lights save you from breaking your neck, and in the guard-room they burn all night; but these do not give enough light for reading or writing.

But this is suppertime, and no one is thinking about work. Presently a minstrel stands up in the middle of the hall to sing some of his own French songs. Since he composes as well as performs he ranks as a gentleman and sits above the salt; though only just above it, for he is not in the first flight of artists. He has been with the Countess all summer, and most of his poems are familiar; he will move on before winter and someone else will come in his place, so that the family may keep in touch with all the new movements in literature.

In poetry fashions are changing. The elaborate songs of the troubadours, with their intricate meter, their savage satire, and their contemporary political allusions, no longer please. Perhaps they have been found too difficult, for to understand them the audience must do nearly as much work as the poet. Instead the minstrels relate anecdotes: either thrilling melodramas of the supernatural which may be compared with the science fiction of the present day, or love stories such as are now published in magazines which are aimed at a feminine public. These stories are often set in the timeless world of King Arthur, which has the advantage that it is peopled with recognizable ready-made characters: Sir Lancelot, Sir Kay, Sir Perceval. These heroes remain always the same age, though the adventure should last for several years; they have no money worries and no political aims. The obvious parallel in our own literature is the "western."

The great advantage of these modern tales is that no one can quarrel over them. Everyone is in favor of the Holy Grail and against Sir Mordred; whereas a *sirvente*, or satirical song, composed by the troubadour Bertrand de Born on the subject of King Richard the Lion-Hearted might have led to a free fight nearly every time it was sung.

Though the household listen politely they are a little bored with this familiar stuff. When the minstrel has finished there are more novel entertainers. A traveler has turned up with a dancing bear. They perform their turn, and the Countess sends down to them a suitable present. Before they go out to sleep in a corner of the courtyard the trainer passes around a bowl to collect a little more from the general company.

Sitting in a lowly place is a professional pilgrim, who spends his life wandering from shrine to shrine. In the spring he left Compostela in Spain to go by way of Canterbury to St. Patrick's Purgatory in Ireland. He expects a meal and a bed at any Christian house where he may choose to stop, and of course he gets them in this great castle. Now he stands up to tell of his journeys, as some payment to his generous hosts.

At the high table they do not listen very closely. This pilgrim is an ignorant uneducated rustic, and his mother tongue is an unfamiliar English dialect. They can hardly understand what he is saying, and he tells them nothing about the wars of the Kings of Navarre and Aragon, which might have been interesting. Some of the recent miracles of St. James are mildly amusing, and the splendors of the tomb of St. Thomas at Canterbury will always bear retelling. But they are unlucky to have to listen to such a dull man, though a holy one. The reminiscences of a returned crusader would be much more rewarding.

By our ideas it is still early when the Countess rises from the table and gives the signal for bed; but tomorrow all these people are going to get up before sunrise. To stay awake in the gloomy half-light of the torches is not much fun, and it would be stupid to waste daylight by lying in bed after dawn. To keep awake until midnight, as we do every time we go to the theater, was then a rare exploit, something for the rake or the drunkard to boast about long afterward.

The children go immediately to their beds. Half an hour later a watchman walks around the whole castle, to

58

make sure that every fire is properly banked. In the days of flint and tinder the fire in a hearth would not be completely extinguished at night because of the bother of kindling it again in the morning; instead the live coals must be covered with ashes or earth. Careless or chilly people sometimes leave a fire uncovered, which is dangerous. This watchman's round is the curfew, or "cover-fire," which we sometimes suppose was an order for lights out. It was not that exactly. You might sit up afterward, so long as your fire was safely banked.

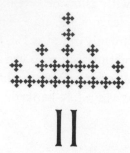

# II

## THE FAMILY OF A COUNTRY KNIGHT

As we have seen, the Earl's family is always on the move, between Sussex, Yorkshire, and Wales. By contrast the family we shall now consider, with three children of the same ages and bearing the same names, never travels outside the bounds of its own Midland county.

We are still dealing with the upper class. If Sir William, the father of this family, should happen to visit the Earl he would be placed above the salt. If there were not many visitors at the castle he might even be placed at the high table; for a good herald could show that he is a kinsman of the Earl, through a daughter of the first Norman Earl who married a lesser baron and bore daughters who married into the minor gentry. Though for two hundred years their forebears have lived in England, neither family forgets that they owe their position to the Norman Conquest.

Sir William holds less land than the Earl. But the big difference, which affects their whole lives, is that Sir William's land lies all in one neighborhood. Not that he holds one knight's fee—the amount of land imposing the obligation of knight service—from one lord; that tidy arrangement of the original Conqueror began to break up as soon as it had been made, when the original occupants gave portions of land to their younger sons, to their daughters, or to religious houses. Sir William holds seven-eighths of one knight's fee, five-eighths of another, and three-sixteenths of a third; in addition he has odd scattered plowlands in several villages. But all his land lies within ten miles of his house. The estate, though it is held from three different lords, is managed as a unit, with its own mill and forge and dovecote.

Sir William has never performed personal knight service in the retinue of any one of his lords; he prefers to offer money in lieu. But he owns all the equipment of a knight, complete armor and weapons and a rather elderly destrier, and he knows how to use them. Once or twice he has been called out by the sheriff to take his place in the shire-levy which descends from the old Saxon fyrd, or assembly of the militia. But that was in the bad old days, when Simon de Montfort was fighting King Henry III. Now the civil wars are finished, and he never expects to bear arms again.

The home of this family, their manor house, is something between a small castle and a large farmsteading. At one end is a square stone tower three stories high, with a flat embattled roof. Adjoining it is the hall, also of stone, whose gabled roof lies level with the third story of the tower. At the end nearer the tower an upper floor affords little bedchambers and a solar for the lord, but at the farther end the hall rises clear to the timbered roof. At this far end of the hall a screened-off passage cuts the house in two; beyond it lie the kitchen, stillroom, and dairy, of timber and plaster on a stone base. At right angles to these are the stable and cowhouse, of flimsy wattle-and-daub without even a stone footing. A ditch and bank, crowned with a thick thorn hedge, surround the whole building. If raiders should come when there are plenty of men on the place the hedge might be held against a petty attack; if the raiders break in to drive off the cattle the family might be saved by taking refuge in the fireproof stone tower. But if a real army should march that way Sir William would not be so foolhardy as to attempt resistance.

Everyone rises at dawn, as in the Earl's castle. But there are not nearly so many people in this smaller house. Since the three rooms in the tower are used only for storage, the upper floor over one end of the hall is divided into a chamber for Sir William and his wife, two others for the boys and their sister, and the little solar. The partitions between these rooms are flimsy boards, so that if the household should vary in size the four chambers can easily be made into three or five. Of course in one room you can hear anything said in any of the others, but the family are used to living without privacy.

In Ralph and Roger's little cubbyhole there is no furniture except two narrow beds. Their clothes hang from horizontal bars jutting from the wall. Their mattresses are of canvas stuffed with straw; for bedclothes they have blankets only, without sheets. In the whole house there is only one grand bed, set against the stone outer wall under a permanent canopy and curtains; their parents sleep in it, under linen sheets and woolen blankets and one fur coverlet.

It would be wrong for a young lady to sleep entirely by herself. Anne shares her room with her old nurse, who was a young peasant widow when first she came to the manor to look after the baby girl. Twelve years in good service have taught Mistress Alice some of the manners of the gentry. When Anne goes out in public (but this does not happen often) her nurse can go with her and pass unnoticed in any company.

At dawn everyone is getting dressed. They wear clothes of the same general type as those worn in the Earl's castle, but of rougher material and more serviceable cut. The boys' sleeveless surcoats are of thick serge, dyed dark blue, for the herb called woad is the cheapest and most easily procured dye. Anne and her mother, Madam Margaret, wear short kirtles, which they can hitch up even shorter by pulling them through their plain, narrow girdles. Over their shoes the women put on pattens, wooden platform soles fastened with a sandal strap; the boys wear boots which end just above the ankle. The yard behind the house is trampled daily by horses and cows so that it is always muddy, even in August.

Sir William dresses more carefully, for today he has an important public engagement. He puts on hose of saffron yellow and a green tunic (dyes for these two colors are not expensive), and instead of a surcoat a *garde-corps*. This is a loose outdoor garment put on over the head and reaching well below the knee. A hood hangs loose at the back. The wide sleeves are longer than the wearer's arms, so that they may cover his hands in cold weather; but in front each sleeve is slit between shoulder and elbow so that with his arms through the slits and the sleeves hanging empty the wearer may use his hands unencumbered. Sir William's *garde-corps* is of gray unbleached wool; it is worn to keep out the weather, not to look smart. Since it has no girdle it hangs loose. He and his sons wear plain linen coifs, clean but without ornament.

The men wash at the trough in the yard, but the ladies find warm water and clean towels in the kitchen. The maidservants are too busy to spend their time carrying washbasins up the stairs to the bedchambers. These stairs are a steep ladderlike gangway, which can easily be removed for repair by the local carpenter. They would never be removed as a measure of defense, because no one would seek refuge from enemies in the flimsy upper story with its inflammable partitions and floor.

A little crucifix stands on a chest in a corner of the hall. For a few minutes the whole family kneel in prayer before it, while Sir William leads them in muttered Our

64

Fathers and Hail Marys. He would like to hear Mass every morning, not only because that is how great noblemen live but because he is genuinely devout. But he cannot afford a private chaplain, and the parish church is a mile away across the fields. Besides, the parish priest does not offer Mass on every weekday, and you never can be sure on which mornings he will decide to sleep late. They say he drinks; but he is not a scandalous drunkard against whom the Bishop could take action, and he always turns up in time for Mass on Sundays and great feasts. Sir William, the patron of the living, who appointed him, would look foolish if he complained to the rural dean about his own priest.

After prayers they all sit at the high table, under the solar at the end of the hall, to eat the bread and ale Roger has fetched from the screens. The bread is slightly gray, because oats have been mixed with the wheat; but the ale is strong and good, freshly brewed from their own barley. They eat a rather bigger breakfast than did the castle-dwellers, for they will do more strenuous work during the day; in winter they sometimes eat bowls of hot porridge, but it would be greedy to begin a fine August day with such solid food.

"The screens," from which Roger fetched the family breakfast, is in many ways the center of the house. There is nothing there to sit on, and no one idles there, but it is an important crossroads. The screen proper, of painted planks, is fixed a few feet in front of the far end of the hall. It is pierced by three doorways, side by side. That on the left leads, through a corresponding door in the far wall, to the pantry, a small room where all the bread is kept; the center door faces a short passage leading to the kitchen; the door on the right gives access to the buttery, another small room, exactly balancing the pantry, in which are kept the pitchers of ale drawn from the casks in the cellar and ready to serve.

These service doors are only half the function of "the screens." Closing the left end of the screens-passage, set in the end of the side wall of the hall, is the front door of the whole house, a stout nail-studded thickness of oak which stands open from dawn to dusk. Facing it at the right end of the passage stands the back door, leading to the yard and stable. This is normally unbarred during daylight, but it is divided horizontally and only the upper half stands open; the lower half is kept latched so that Madam Margaret may notice whenever anyone comes in or goes out. Etiquette decrees that all servants, visitors of the lower class, and men carrying supplies for the kitchen shall enter by the back door. The front door is reserved for visiting gentry and the family.

This arrangement ensures that there will always be a through draft in the screens-passage, which often penetrates into the hall. In winter it can be very tiresome. But it also ensures that anyone entering the hall will attract attention. In an unfortified manor that is a wise precaution.

The morning is chilly. For a few minutes the family warm themselves at the central fire in the hall, which smolders day and night all the year round; the smoke escapes, after blackening the rafters of the roof, through an opening in the stone tiles. When the hall was built, a generation ago, there was talk of putting a chimney in one of the long walls at the side; but that would not have warmed the whole room evenly. This central hearth fills the air with smoke, but a dozen people can hold out their hands to it at the same time.

One by one the family slip away to the privies in the stable yard. There are two of these little wooden cabins, one for men and one for women. They have no drainage of any kind, but from time to time a servant removes the filth in a big tub. These cabins are reserved for the use of the gentry only; a little way off is another cabin for the female servants, but menservants and farm workers have the whole wide world for a privy.

The head groom brings around Sir William's better hackney, and Sir William prepares to set out on his journey. Then there is a hitch. The second groom, who should ride with him as horse-holder and attendant, is needed at home to look after a sick cow. There are only two full-time grooms on the manor, though at busy times they may call on plentiful unskilled help. But the second groom takes charge of all sick animals; he has a knack of getting medicine down their throats through a cow's horn, and he knows a number of helpful spells. He is now mixing a draught, while he mutters to himself a long rigmarole which will make this cow calve easily. (Of course there were murmurs of magic when this groom first came to the manor. But the parish priest investigated, and pronounced his spells to be genuine petitions to God and the saints, not invocations of the Devil.)

Sir William is at a loss. A respectable knight cannot ride unattended, as though he were a vagabond; when he gets to the meeting he cannot leave his hackney tied to a tree. He decides to take Ralph with him. The boy is fourteen, old enough to act as a squire. His manners are adequate for any company, and it is time he began to learn the duties which will fall on him when his father is dead.

Delighted by the unexpected break in routine, Ralph changes into riding boots which reach halfway up his calf. For a long day in the saddle he ought to wear padded hose as well, but he has none; he grows too fast to have many clothes. The stirrup leathers will chafe his legs, but for such an interesting ride it is worth it. Best of all, he is to carry his father's sword. He comes down from the tower with the long leather scabbard hanging diagonally across his back, the hilt appearing behind his left shoulder. That proves that the sword is carried as luggage, not as his personal weapon; the neighbors might grumble if a young boy went about wearing the sword of a knight. When Sir William dismounts at the end of his ride he will buckle the sword around his waist. His gilded spurs display his rank, but when acting officially in his capacity as knight he ought to have a sword about him. If he were younger he would ride with it, but he finds that it bumps against his gouty leg.

Ralph has no *garde-corps* for traveling, so he must

keep warm in his sleeveless surcoat; instead of a hood he puts over his coif a round pudding-shaped felt hat. The dagger at his girdle is meant for cutting food and for all the other things we do with a pocketknife; but he may think of himself as an armed escort, even after he has given over the knightly sword to his father.

He rides the second hackney, normally his mother's. The only other good horse in the stable is Sir William's destrier, which is daily exercised by a groom on foot. It is much too valuable to be ridden on casual journeys over rough roads. Five years ago Sir William gave sixty pounds for him, the largest sum of money he has ever paid out for anything. The hackneys are worth two or three pounds apiece; the half-dozen common nags in the stable, for riding about the demesne and carrying messages, could be bought at any fair for ten or fifteen shillings.

When you buy a destrier you pay for his long training. He must gallop straight, turn handily, never shy or flinch when weapons are brandished near his eyes. Of course he is also much bigger than the hackneys, a weight-carrier who can gallop under a knight in full mail. If Sir William were a better horseman he might train his own destriers, and perhaps make money by breeding them for sale. But for all his knighthood he is by choice a farmer, and by necessity occupied much of the time with local affairs. He would never go to the wars of his own free will; yet if he cannot produce mail and destrier at the muster the sheriff might fine him for neglecting his duty.

On the little local road which leads through the manor, a ribbon of mud and ruts which has never been surfaced or repaired, father and son ride side by side; though when they reach the King's highway Ralph will have to keep a length behind his lord. As they ride Sir William explains the business on which he has been summoned.

"It's the most tiresome form of jury service," he complains, "and the third time in less than a year that it has come my way. But that's how it goes. In this county there aren't enough knights for all the inquests the King orders us to decide. In the old days a yeoman who could afford horse and arms was eager to be dubbed knight. Now they find that being ranked as a gentleman takes up too much of their time. They ought to be compelled to be knighted if they hold land enough. They say the King is thinking of ordering them to do it, and making them pay a fine if they refuse. But of course the King will be better pleased if they are obstinate and pay up than if they obey him. That's another of the troubles of this degenerate age: the King is always in such need of money that anyone may break the law if he is willing to pay for it. But there it is. We are a knightly family, and must maintain our station in life.

"I wish they hadn't picked on me for this particular case," he goes on. "I said it was the worst form of jury service, and so it is. A criminal trial isn't so bad. If you find the man guilty he is hanged; that's the end of him, and he can't seek revenge on you. Or you find him not guilty, and he is grateful to you for the rest of his life. You end with either a living friend or a dead enemy, which is fair enough. But this is a case of inheritance, and a tricky one. There was a knight who lived to a very great age, until all his children were dead. But he left heirs, two of them. One is the son of his daughter, the other the daughter of his son. Now, young Ralph, which of them do you think ought to have grandfather's land?"

"Well, sir, the man always inherits before the woman. So I suppose the grandson must inherit before the granddaughter."

"Not so fast, my boy. What you mean is that the brother inherits before the sister, and you are right. But if the brother is the heir his claim must pass to his daughter. The grandson traces his descent only through the female line."

"I see. In that case the lady gets the land, though it seems odd to prefer an heiress before a man. Is that what you have decided? Why did you have to make the decision? Is the land under your lordship?"

"Indeed not. When you succeed to my manor you won't be bothered with tenants by knight service, I'm glad to say. They are more trouble than they are worth. I have to decide as a member of the jury. The parties brought suit in the King's court, and the King's judges commanded the sheriff to pick a local jury to decide on the facts. That's why it is so tiresome. Personally I think the granddaughter has the better right, but there are arguments on the other side. If we decide for the grandson no one will be scandalized. But whichever way the verdict goes we shall make enemies."

"Enemies who may fight us?" asks Ralph with a gleam

in his eye. "Do you give your verdict today? Is that why you commanded me to come with you?"

"If they have any sense they won't fight us. We are the King's jury. You can't beat the King; in the long run even Simon de Montfort couldn't. No, they won't fight. But there are other ways of revenging yourself. They can harry me in the sheriff's court, or even before the King's judges. They can bring false accusations—or true ones, for no one observes the law in its entirety all the time. One day a knight of the injured faction may find himself on a jury which has to decide something important to me or my friends. Thank Heaven we don't give our verdict today. This is just a formal meeting to inspect the disputed land, so that we know exactly what both sides claim. We shall talk over our decision, of course, and make sure we are all agreed. Then we shall put off the final verdict for as long as we can, in the hope that one claimant will die or get interested in some other topic or make up the quarrel. It's just possible that we may never be called on to decide the suit."

Ralph is struck with a bright idea which seems to him so excellent that he must tell it to his father at once, though by rights he should speak only when spoken to.

"Look here, sir, how would this do? If the granddaughter has the better right I suppose the jury will decide for her. Let the grandson know that the suit will go against him when it comes to a final decision. But if you can manage it let the granddaughter suppose that her cause is still doubtful. Suggest that she buy off her cousin

73

by offering him a portion of the land. The grandson will be satisfied with very little, since he knows the jury will give him nothing. The granddaughter will be glad to avoid a judgment which might go against her. The parties come to an agreement. The jury never delivers a formal verdict. And you make no enemies."

His father looks at him steadily. "That's just what we shall do, of course. I told you the story carefully, hoping you would see the way of escape. One day you will be in my place as a knight of the shire, and they will always be putting you on a jury or telling you to pronounce your opinion without fear or favor. When that time comes, remember that you have sworn to tell the truth. It would be disgraceful if a knight were to conceal his opinion for fear of his enemies. But you need not go out of your way to make enemies. If you are careful you need never reach the formal verdict. Let it leak out beforehand and the parties will compromise. The other thing to bear in mind is this: never let a suitor go away utterly empty-handed, if you think he had an arguable case. It's more important to avoid starting a feud than to see justice done to the uttermost farthing. Our first duty is to keep the peace. Only when that is secure may we go on to render to every man his due."

Roger, like his brother, spends the morning in helping his father. Since there is no bailiff the peasants of the manor work on the demesne under the orders of their reeve, a fellow peasant chosen by themselves. To make things more complicated, there are in all three reeves, representing the main holding and the two outlying portions which in Domesday Book, the record of the survey of the lands of England ordered by William the Conqueror, are written as separate manors. Harvest is approaching, and the work will have to be organized so that the wagons and teams (there are never enough of them) will not be wanted in three places at once. The reeves, jealous of their authority, will never agree among themselves unless someone from the big house presides over their meeting. After breakfast Roger finds the three peasants waiting for him in the muddy stable yard. He tells them that the fields will be reaped in the same order as last year, and that the owner of every team called away to work on another manor will be paid a halfpenny a day for its use. That is the common-sense solution, which they have been expecting. But as they carry it into effect they can grumble that it was forced on them by the gentry, and that if left to themselves they would have done everything differently.

At ten years of age Roger can tell a fit horse or ox from a sick one. In the same way he can tell whether a field has been well cultivated or neglected. When he has finished with the reeves he makes a point of looking at every field and every animal on the demesne.

For this he takes out from the stable a rough little moorland pony, and saddles it himself. As the pony ambles around the headlands he slouches in his seat, with a loose rein and a bent knee. He can manage the knightly style of riding for a short time, if he has to; but he is not going to be a knight when he grows up, and this un-

75

gentlemanly way of sitting is more comfortable on the grass-fed pony.

Roger's real bent is for farming and estate management. He genuinely likes to see two ears of wheat growing where only one grew before. Yet in the normal course of events he will never hold any land of his own; all must go to his elder brother, so that Ralph may keep up the style of living appropriate to his birth. However, there is a way out. Roger and his parents are agreed on his future: when he is five or six years older he will apply for admittance to a nearby Benedictine monastery.

St. Milborough's is an ancient and wealthy foundation, but now out of fashion and short of recruits. In King Canute's day it held forty choirmonks besides novices, and the endowments are still amply sufficient for those numbers. At present, the monks complain, every young man who longs to serve God goes off to join these newfangled friars, who advise kings and lecture in universities and preach missions to slum parishes and in general mix with the secular world more freely than any cloistered monk would dream of doing. Consequently, in the foundation there are only twenty-eight choirmonks, which means that in practice only a score of brethren are left to sing the Office in choir.

For, and this is the core of Roger's plan for his future, the wide estates of the abbey need full-time agents to look after them. Out of the twenty-eight monks in the establishment eight are employed on special duties, and therefore excused the burden of attendance in choir. The Office occupies eight hours out of the twenty-four and makes it impossible to travel any distance from the chapel. These eight monks, known as the obedientiaries, are the prior, cellarer, sacristan, and almoner, who have special duties in any monastery, and the four bailiffs in distant manors. They are elected by the community in chapter, nominally for three years but in practice for life, and the usual course of promotion is by seniority from junior bailiff to prior. (The abbot is appointed for life by the King, and is often a stranger from another monastery.)

Not every choirmonk is eager for an obedience, an appointment which will take him from his religious duties. Some are truly devout or scholarly; others are afraid of having to add up accounts. If Roger enters the monastery at eighteen he may take his full vows a year later; by the time he is twenty-five he could be a full-time farmer and man of business, with regular promotion in prospect for the rest of his life.

He will have to make sacrifices, especially at the outset. A novice is a very lowly form of religious life, set to menial duties and perhaps beaten if he does not perform them to the satisfaction of his superiors. At the end of the year of probation, when he takes his vows, he will have to give up all thought of marriage or of any other form of feminine companionship. St. Milborough's is slack, but it is not actively corrupt; the brethren keep their vow of chastity, though sometimes they fail in obedience and they know ways of dodging the full consequence of the vow of poverty.

During his years as a choirmonk, while he is waiting

for his first obedience, he will live a hard life. Never enough sleep, with one Office at midnight and the next before dawn; never a taste of meat, which is forbidden in the refectory; dirty and threadbare clothing winter and summer, with no extra tunic to keep out the cold and no chance to take off his voluminous cowl during a heat wave. These clothes, incidentally, are worn day and night, in bed, in the cloister, in choir; though if the monastery is run as it should be, clean clothing will be issued once a month. During his spare time—but he will have little spare time—he must complete his education and prepare for ordination to the priesthood. He will enjoy one hour of recreation a day, when he may talk to the other monks; in winter he may pass this hour warming himself by the fire if the abbot, who lives in a separate and comfortable lodging, thinks it is cold enough to light the fire in the calefactory.

A very hard life of constant discipline and watchfulness; but no harder than that of a soldier on active service. A man of knightly birth should be able to stand it, as his cousins endure the hard work and meager living of pages in a strange castle. After a few years of this, if all goes well, he will get his first obedience, and then good-by to hardship. As obedientiary in charge of a manor he will be excused attendance at Office; for much of the time he will live in a distant grange where, if he is discreet about it, he may get up when he likes in the morning and eat beef for the sake of his health. He will exercise all the rights of a lord over the local peasants.

As time goes on he will be promoted to some duty

in the monastery, where he will probably have a private lodging and a private kitchen for his private meals. If he is willing and competent the community may in due course elect him their prior. Then he may be as much or as little of a monk as he chooses, taking his place in choir and in the refectory whenever he feels like it, and retiring to his private apartments on the plea of pressure of business whenever he prefers to be alone.

That is not the end of the career open to him, though it is as far as his brethren at St. Milborough's can send him. A willing, efficient prior may attract the attention of the King. One day he may be appointed abbot, probably of another monastery. Strictly speaking, the King will do no more than recommend him to the community for election, since the community have enjoyed the right to elect their abbot since St. Benedict drew up the Rule by which they live; but monks never defy the expressed wishes of the King.

The abbot of a great monastery is as important as any baron. In fact the law sees him chiefly as a baron, feudal lord of all the possessions of the abbey, entitled if he chooses to lead the abbey's knights to battle. If he stays at home he will live in his own comfortable lodging, quite distinct from the monks' quarters. He will entertain his chosen guests at his private table, where the menu will have been chosen by himself. At this period the separation of abbot and community has gone so far that monastic writers recommend an abbot to invite his choir-monks to dinner from time to time, so that he may get to know them personally.

But for long periods an abbot is absent from home. He is summoned as of right to every meeting of the King's great council, which is in process of becoming the House of Lords; he will attend any synods or local church councils in his own part of the country. He may be sent to Rome on the business of his community, or to some foreign court on a diplomatic mission for the King.

Benedictine abbots hold office for life, and there are not very many of them. But Roger's hope of achieving the rank is not absurd. The Church offers a career open to talent from any station in life; but other things being equal, monks prefer to be ruled by a gentleman. His good manners will help him, his interest in agriculture, and the self-discipline he shows in seeking an education when he might be enjoying himself. In the spiritual life he will never be a great leader; but in the community under his care saints and scholars will enjoy adequate food, weathertight dwellings, and no money worries, while they get on with their more important work.

There is no doubt that St. Milborough's will accept him as a novice. He is just the kind of recruit they look for: a gentleman, and therefore used to living in a crowd without bothering his neighbors; a worker, with enough tenacity of purpose to obey the rules he has accepted of his own free will; second son of a substantial landholder, who will bring a handy little dowry when he enters the community and may, if his elder brother should meet with a fatal accident, bring in addition his father's whole flourishing manor.

As regards the inheritance of his father's land the law

interposes an obstacle. A monk is dead to the secular world, and therefore in the eyes of the law he is a dead man who cannot inherit anything. All the same, if Ralph should die after Roger has taken his vows Sir William would be in theory sonless, and would probably make a will leaving his land to St. Milborough's.

Roger will be welcome. He is entering the life of religion not to pray, not because he loves God, but because he wants to farm and has no land of his own. But he will keep the rules and give no scandal. He knows what he must do without, and considers the sacrifice worth while. He will go far, and die a respected abbot.

Anne spends the morning helping her mother with the housekeeping. In the manor house this is not merely a matter of supervision, as in the Earl's castle. Madam Margaret works with her own hands, while Anne and her nurse Mistress Alice fetch and carry for her. Not that there are no servants; but they are clumsy and untrained. The cook can be trusted with roasts and pies; anything more complicated, fancy cakes, subtleties, confections of almonds and raisins, must be made by the ladies of the house. There is no spacious flower garden; roses from the straggling bushes in the yard must be distilled into scent, a tricky job which is the specialty of Mistress Alice. The maids mend linen and clothing, but fine sewing and embroidery are the province of Madam Margaret. There is no clerk of the kitchen to keep track of supplies and suppress waste; the lady of the house must give out the milk and cheese and butter which come in daily from the demesne, decide when to slaughter another ox or sheep, apportion the flour for baking. The servants are not only untrained, they are not completely honest. That is to say, they would never steal anything valuable, money or a silver cup; but if they get the chance they will sell or give to their friends any food or stores or clothing that they think will not be missed. If Madam Margaret should relax her control the cost of housekeeping would quickly double.

There are many tasks about the place which must be supervised by someone responsible, now that Sir William and Ralph have gone away for the day. The mews, a dark little shed beside the stable, contains three goshawks and a peregrine. A boy cleans out the floor and carries in food and straw, but he is not a trained falconer and must be told what to do. Every day the hawks must be inspected, to make sure they are healthy; they ought to be taken out daily on the wrist if they are not to forget their training.

Sir William, naturally, does not keep a pack of hounds, since he is not allowed to hunt even over his own land. But he is permitted to catch rabbits and hares, and there is always vermin to be kept down, foxes and badgers and weasels. Wandering about the yard, not in very good condition, are a few greyhounds and terriers. There are also a couple of watchdogs, big fierce beasts which are kept chained in the daytime. They are descended from the hounds which killed the last wolf in these parts, sixty or seventy years ago. Sometimes Anne dreams that another wolf will appear for her to hunt; they are reported to be plentiful in Scotland.

All these animals ought to be looked over every day by some member of the family; horses and oxen and sheep also need daily care.

Dinner is served soon after eleven, earlier than in the castle. It is a curious fact that the hour of dinner has moved steadily later throughout recorded history, and that it has always been fashionable to dine later than the average.

Anne takes off the kerchief which covered her hair while she was working in the kitchen and yard; Roger changes his boots for low shoes of supple sheepskin; they and their mother, as befits gentlefolk, take great care to appear at the table scrupulously clean. But no one puts on fine clothes for this workaday meal.

At the high table there are only these three and the parish priest, who comes up to the manor on most days to teach Roger in the afternoon. Dinner is the main part of his pay, though Sir William also gives him a few pennies from time to time. Father Andrew is of peasant stock; the children have been warned to copy his Latin but not his table manners. But he has to wash his hands carefully before offering Mass, which ensures that at least part of him is reasonably clean. He wears a long tunic of unbleached wool, like any other prosperous peasant; but he is marked as a priest by his tonsure, which shows up with great effect in his tousled hair.

In deference to Father Andrew, whose French is weak, conversation at the high table is in Midland English. Everyone speaks it easily and naturally, except that Madam Margaret sometimes fumbles for a word. She does this deliberately, to support the fiction that Anglo-French is the normal household language; as of course it ought to be, in the family of a knight whose ancestors came over with the Conqueror.

The real truth is that, though Madam Margaret and Sir William speak French as their mother tongue, their children do not. They can stumble along in it, and every evening they are compelled to speak it to their parents; but the pressure of the English they hear spoken all around them has overwhelmed their ancestral tongue. Except when a visitor of good birth comes to the manor, and that does not happen very often, everyone except their parents speaks English to them.

This is something new. Sir William's father understood very little English, so that his upper servants had to speak French to him; but then many of these upper servants had been born in the French possessions of the kings of England. But seventy years ago King John was driven out of Normandy, and Henry III was unlucky in his Continental campaigns, so that now King Edward holds no land beyond the Channel except Gascony, where they speak Languedoc instead of North French. There is less social intercourse between England and France than there used to be, now that no one holds land in both countries.

A point which we often forget is that no spoken language stands still. My readers do not talk exactly as their grandparents talked when they were children; if I had been writing this book sixty years ago I should have phrased much of it differently. In the same way the French of England changed from one generation to another; but because Englishmen seldom visited France they did not become aware of the changes which were modifying Continental French. The two descendants of one language grew farther apart until, 120 years later, in the reign of King Richard II, French officials arranging a truce with English envoys complained that they could not understand these Englishmen when they spoke what they called French.

By that time Anglo-French had become the private dialect of the English nobility. It barely lingered into the sixteenth century, though lawyers continued to write in it until well into the seventeenth. In the later thirteenth century the change is just beginning. The children of the Earl in the first chapter will speak French to their own children after they are grown up; but these children of a country knight, compelled to speak French only on formal occasions, will not bother to teach it to the next generation.

Besides the high table there are two long tables running down the hall, with a great many people sitting at them. Anyone who is entitled to dine in the hall does so, even if he has a cozy home of his own. Fuel is scarce. To burn good timber would be wasteful; coal is too awkward and heavy to be carried far by land, though it is beginning to reach London by sea; peat is used where it can be found, but it is not common in England. The normal fuel is the brushwood which springs up in a forest after the big trees have been felled; there is not enough of it to keep many cooking fires burning.

So all the farm servants crowd into the hall, and their wives as well if they can leave the children. An advantage of working at the manor is that you get a cooked dinner every day; in the cottages round about they cook only on Sundays, and on other days make do with cold bacon and stale bread.

There is no symbolic saltcellar; any gentry who should visit the manor would be placed at the high table. But the head groom and the head cowman are persons of importance, and each presides over a table.

This establishment does not eat a whole ox every day, as they did in the castle. The main dish at the high table today is beef stew, recooked from the roast beef they had on Sunday. For even though they are careful with meat they must kill an ox when they want beef. Outside the towns there are no butchers' shops; if countrymen want to eat meat at all they must kill an animal and eat it until it is finished.

There is only one course. Besides the beef stew it includes mutton pies, pork sausages, and a big platter holding a dozen roast pigeons. Sir William's dovecote stands in the stable yard, important both as a sign of lordship and as a source of fresh meat in winter; only the lord of a manor may keep pigeons, which of course feed on his tenants' grain. Today's dinner contains no chickens; the hungry athletic hens who scratch about the yard are valued rather as a source of eggs than as themselves worth eating.

The lesser servants at the lower end of the long tables do not dine on beef. They are given a little, rather as seasoning than as food, and they fill up on butter and cheese. Everyone has an unstinted amount of rye bread.

Before Madam Margaret there stands a horn cup, banded with silver at rim and foot. She pours wine from a leather flagon, but does not fill the capacious cup. Everyone else, including her children, drinks ale. Madam Margaret alone has a manchet of dark rye bread.

But though there is no luxury everyone is happy. This is the peak of the day. They have plenty to eat because they have worked the land and cared for their animals, and because no armed men have come to carry off their store. It might easily have been different. Old men can remember seasons of famine; every adult can remember the plundering bands of the Barons' War. Today's dinner has been earned by hard work. Now they may relax before going off to earn tomorrow's.

At the high table Madam Margaret and Father Andrew discuss farming and the future. The harvest promises to be bigger than ever, because more land has been taken into cultivation. Trouble will come when there is no more waste to be opened to the plow. Before that happens Father Andrew is sure something will turn up, perhaps a new town with room for extra people such as have recently been founded in Wales, perhaps an epidemic to thin out the population. There will be something, never fear; because it is God's plan that the village should feed the men of the village.

At that time everyone who thought about the future assumed a stable population. Thirty years hence there ought to be exactly as many peasants as now to till the soil, exactly as many knights to protect them. Of course things did not work out in that way. The thirteenth century seems to have been a period of expansion, with many towns founded and villages growing larger. Married couples had a great many children; but a number of these children died in infancy, and many adults, priests and monks and nuns, did not marry. Nonetheless, pressure on the land increased from about 1250 to 1348; then, before village could collide with village after plowing up all the waste, came the catastrophe of the Black Death. Some villages disappeared and have never since been inhabited; in others, holdings went begging for lack of peasants to till them until the land enclosures of the sixteenth century.

All this lies in the future. At the moment things are improving. Next winter the village will have enough to eat, and Sir William will be somewhat richer than the year before.

But it looks as though he will have less time for farming. In their discussion Madam Margaret and Father Andrew have now turned to the increasing burden of local government. Young King Edward's remedy for every trouble is to impanel a jury of local knights to inquire into the facts of the case; more of these juries are set up every time the judges come down on circuit, and there are just not enough knights to go around.

Respectable landholders of yeoman stock are reluctant to take up knighthood. One reason is the increasing cost of knightly equipment. At Hastings Sir William's shadowy ancestor rode an ordinary horse; he wore a steel cap and a shirt of linked mail, and carried lance, sword, and a plain leather shield. Sir William's destrier cost him sixty pounds at Smithfield horse market, and in five years at the longest he will have to buy another; his armor is so heavy, with plate over mail on his arms and legs and a steel cuirass under his heraldic surcoat, that only a very fine horse can carry him. His shield is a costly work of art, correctly blazoned by a skilled heraldic painter. His close helm represents a month's work by a highly paid armorer. His lance is a long straight spar of sound timber, and yet so easily broken that he must have half a dozen spares as well. The latest fashion is to have your coat of arms embroidered on your surcoat, instead of merely painted; that will be an additional expense when Ralph is knighted.

The other reason yeomen are reluctant to become knights is simply the new burden of local duties. In the whole county there are only about fifty knights who can always be found at home, and fifteen of this small number are too old or infirm to undertake responsible work. Yet there are often six juries in the field at one time, so that every juryman is doing two jobs at once.

Jurymen are compelled to swear an oath before they begin, though no one likes to take oath if it can be avoided. God-fearing men dread the mortal sin of perjury, and everyone thinks it undignified to be *compelled* to swear. If there were no oath it would be easier to compose local quarrels; but the King insists on getting to the bottom of each case, no matter how much bad feeling that may cause. Above all, the waste of time is resented. No knight has suggested asking for payment; landholding knights have always served the King without pay. But now he is demanding too much service.

On the other hand, it is pleasant to have a finger in every local pie, to be known in the shire court as a man of weight and influence. There is talk of reviving an old scheme of Montfort's: to fetch up two country knights from every shire to confer with the barons of the King's council about national affairs. If the plan comes to anything Sir William is sure to be chosen to represent his county, and a journey to court on the King's business would be most enjoyable. Besides, as Father Andrew points out, if Sir William were unwilling to serve, Sir John from over the hill would probably be chosen in his place; and to yield place to Sir John would be more than Sir William could bear.

Dinnertime in the country is not the end of the day's work, though for many of the peasants it is the end of working on the demesne. The diners rise briskly, and go out without lingering. Only Father Andrew remains at the high table; while Roger fetches from a chest in the tower pens, ink, and paper, and a tattered copy of the acts of a provincial council held in France about fifty years ago, the only Latin text of any length which has found its way to this rustic manor.

The pens have been made at home from goose feathers; though there is an art in cutting them correctly and not everyone can do it. The ink was compounded in the still-room of the manor, from oak galls and soot and a few spells. But paper must be bought for cash, and even the crumbling worst quality which Roger uses is fairly expensive. The priest produces a tiny fragment of pumice stone for erasing mistakes; originally it must have come all the way from Mount Etna in Sicily, but it found its way into Father Andrew's wallet while he was waiting in the cloister of St. Milborough's to see the prior.

When he is a monk Roger will speak nothing but Latin, on the rare occasions when conversation is permitted. Learning it is not very difficult; his old-fashioned Anglo-French gives him the meaning of most of the words, and the grammar causes him less trouble because the church Latin of the thirteenth century is made up of phrases rather than single words, a mosaic of passages from the Bible, the missal, and the Fathers. Soon he will know most of the Psalter by heart, and from some psalm he may surely extract a phrase to suit any occasion; if he cannot remember the Latin name for some everyday object, a bridle or a pair of shoes, he may tack a Latin termination onto the French word and everyone will understand.

In reading and writing he has to recognize more signs than the twenty-five letters of the alphabet (I and J counting as one); Latin terminations may be expressed by putting a little squiggle over the last letter of the stem, but these must be accurately traced or the grammar will go awry. These contractions come in handy when you want to put a modern name into Latin and are not sure how to spell it; *Comes Cest'* is the Earl of Chester and *Ep' Wig'* the Bishop of Worcester, which avoids a lot of pen-chewing.

Once Roger gets to St. Milborough's he may continue his education for as long as he likes; one of the few objects a monk, vowed to poverty, was permitted to keep by him was the book he had borrowed from the monastic library. Every work which deals with a serious subject—theology, history, mathematics, geography—is written in Latin. A knowledge of that language is the essential key to learning.

It does not much matter that the manor has only one book, and that a rather irrelevant compilation; Roger can learn Latin from the acts of that French council as easily as from Caesar or Vergil.

To pass the afternoon Anne rides out to look over the sheep. A groom rides with her, not because there is any danger in this quiet Midland countryside but because a young lady should never ride alone. She would have preferred to take out a hawk; but there is not much game to be found in the nearby thickets, and her father says that soon there will be none if his children go hawking every day. Besides, it is not much fun to go hawking alone, and neither of her brothers can go with her.

The sheep are pastured on the waste, the stretch of scrub and rough grassland which surrounds the village and cuts it off from neighboring settlements. Though the waste is uncultivated it is a vital part of the rural economy; everyone knows the precise landmarks which divide his village's waste from that of the next village. From the waste come firewood and peat, rushes for lighting and heather for thatching, fenceposts, and occasionally, with the special permission of Sir William, a whole tree to provide the frame of a peasant's cottage.

The waste is used also for rough grazing, the only grazing on the manor except for the water meadows and the one common field which lies fallow this year. Here the sheep range under the care of Wat the shepherd and his boy. Wat looks after the sheep singlehanded. The boy is there to fetch and carry and run errands to the village, for Wat may stay out on the waste for weeks at a time. He has thrown a piece of canvas over a bush to make a sleeping place, and he keeps his little fire smoldering day and night since it is hard to kindle a light with flint and tinder in the open air. His ordinary food is bread and milk and cheese, which need no cooking.

This is not the kind of life that would suit everybody, but for a poor man it is the only escape from the incessant communal chatter and curiosity of the village. Wat works at his own pace, and seldom has to talk or listen; he does not envy the weary plowman who every evening must sit by the hearth among a crowd of loquacious relatives.

Most of the sheep are Sir William's; but individual

peasants own a few, which are marked by nicks in the ear. Every holding carries limited grazing rights in the waste. Two or three ewes and their lambs are a handy form of savings, because it is fairly easy to turn them into cash. Peasants have no other possessions worth selling; but a sheep can be sold in any weekly market, or killed to make a feast for a wedding or christening. Only an exceptional peasant, of great forethought and self-control, ever builds up a flock of any size.

Sheep are becoming more valuable every day. The market for English wool seems insatiable. Foreign merchants, some of them come all the way from Italy, ride around the country to buy up the annual clip. Sir William would like to increase his grassland. But the waste is already fully stocked and all his plowland in peasant occupation. He might lay down some of his demesne to grass, but then how would he use the labor service his tenants owe to him?

Anne makes herself useful by fetching back to the house a skin of ewe's milk to be made into cheese. On the way home she potters, so as not to arrive before sunset. If she gets back earlier she will be set to do embroidery. It has been a dull day, with her father and elder brother absent.

Anne's future has not yet been decided, though of course she expects that one day she will be married to the man of her father's choice. She will bring no land to her husband, but Sir William will give her a dowry in money besides bedding and other furnishings for her new home. That may be enough to tempt some unambitious household knight. She knows she is not beautiful, for her hair is red. Without land and without exceptional beauty she will never make a good marriage.

If no knight has offered for her by the time she is twenty she may try a nunnery. A nun's is a dull life, but an easy one: say six hours a day in choir and the rest of her time free for gossip. But Anne is too energetic to make a good nun, for in England at that time nuns did no useful work; no nursing or educational work in the world, and very little more study than sufficed to read the Office. Under the Saxon kings Benedictine nunneries had been centers of higher education, the rivals of great monasteries; now, in the thirteenth century, they are mere receptacles for unwanted ladies, where no books are written and even the needlework is not wrought so carefully as it used to be.

Life in a convent holds another danger. An incompetent abbess, completely untrained in administration, may muddle away the revenues until her community literally goes hungry. Sometimes widows and elderly spinsters offer a lump sum, a corody, in return for board and lodging for the remainder of their lives; an abbess desperate for money may accept an insufficient corody for the sake of ready cash, or the boarder may live much longer than expected. Very few English convents have an adequate endowment in land; many of them were founded without adequate funds, to provide a dignified home for some particular dowager. Once the foundress is dead no one takes an interest in the prosperity of the convent. Anne hopes that her father will not command her to become a nun.

There is one unlikely chance of a happy future, so unlikely that she hardly dares to hope for it. She might be given in marriage to a wealthy merchant. A few such marriages have been arranged recently, so she has heard. To live in a town house, small, compact, easy to run, with plenty of money to run it, appeals to Anne as the perfect life. She does not bother to speculate about the character of her future husband, who will in any case be a stranger to her. But Sir William, a knight of ancient lineage and proud of his family, would see any alliance with a merchant as a disgraceful disparagement. Almost certainly her husband will be a poor gentleman; she will pass her married life keeping up appearances on an inadequate income.

Probably Anne will endure a hard-working unhappy future. But for many centuries life has been hard for well-brought-up young ladies who are also poor and plain.

By sunset Sir William and Ralph are home, in good spirits because the lawsuit has been compromised as they desired. Tomorrow for a change Sir William will be at leisure to ride over his own land and supervise the farming. Unfortunately a message has come from the sheriff to say that his services will be needed on the day after that, to inquire into a dispute about the repair of a bridge. The sheriff maintains that it should be repaired, like other bridges, at the cost of the nearest village. The men of the village have appealed to the King's justices in eyre, claiming that the cost of repair should by an ancient charter be borne by the hundreds, or county divisions, on either side of the river. The judges have decided that a jury must inquire into who paid for the last repairs, which probably means going back a century or more. These local duties are a great nuisance, though they are also a tribute to the position and reputation for honest dealing of Sir William.

Supper is plain but substantial: cold beef and cold mutton and plenty of rye bread, with strong ale and sweet mead. The long tables are half empty, for only domestic servants pass the evening in the manor house. Tonight there is no professional entertainment, though if a minstrel or juggler happened to pass that way he would be invited to sing for his supper. When the meal is ended the young people amuse themselves by playing what we would consider nursery games with some of the younger servants. Blind man's buff is a favorite, with its variant, hot cockles, in which the blindfolded victim must guess which hand has delivered a stinging smack on his bottom. To cool off before going to bed they sit around in a circle and compose verses, each in turn rhyming with the verse given by the last speaker.

They go to bed early, ready to rise early for another day of strenuous work on the land.

All day long no one has thought seriously of warfare, although the full equipment of a knight is kept somewhere on the manor. In this Midland county the time has passed when every village must be defended by a trained full-time warrior. If the sheriff or the King should demand his personal service Sir William will ride willingly to the muster; but admittedly a summons to war will be an unwelcome interruption of routine. There is not even a night watchman on guard in the manor. Against casual thieves they trust to the dogs which roam the courtyard, and against armed bandits to the King's Peace.

# III

## THE FAMILY OF A PEASANT

Most of the score or so of great noblemen in England lived like the Earl described in my first chapter, and there were a great many country knights who lived like Sir William in the second. This third chapter is a much more difficult business, because in thirteenth century England it is almost impossible to find a typical peasant.

Some things can be said with a fair measure of certainty. Every peasant was a tenant of a manor, subject to its lord. In the eyes of the law he was a tenant at will, liable to be turned out at any moment for any reason. Instead of paying rent in money for his land he worked on his lord's demesne, and, again in the eyes of the law, his lord fixed the amount of work which must be done for each holding and might vary it at will. Many peasants were serfs, and the word used for this in legal documents was *servus*, which in classical Latin means slave. A serf might be sold or given away, with or without the land to which he was attached. He could not rightfully own property, for everything in his hut, and the hut itself, belonged to the lord who owned him. He might be flogged at the lord's discretion. If he ran away the lord might fetch him back.

That was what the law had to say about the position of a serf. But as in every age, the social conditions of daily life limited the powers granted by law. The lord of a manor who stood on his rights would face trouble from authorities more powerful than he.

The Church saw the serf as a Christian soul, whose salvation was just as important as that of anyone else. He might not be set to work on a Sunday or other great feast on which he was bound to hear Mass. He might not be separated from his wife and young children. To kill him was murder, to defraud him of his just dues one of those grave sins which cry out to Heaven for vengeance. In general, though it was not wrong in itself to be the owner of serfs or slaves, it was believed to be easier to get into Heaven if you had never been tempted to ill-treat helpless inferiors. To free serfs was a work of mercy, which at the Judgment would be set off against your sins.

The King also did something to protect the serf from his lord, not so much from devotion to abstract freedom as from aversion to seeing one of his subjects completely in the power of another. The King's coroner had a duty to inquire into any violent death in his territory; he would inquire into the killing of a serf as willingly as into that of a free man. If the lord had killed him, either of set purpose or by ill-treatment, there would be a charge of murder. Perhaps the lord would claim that he had the right to hang his peasants. Then the King's judges would investigate the matter, and they would investigate very closely. The private right to High Justice did exist in England; but it was rare, and the judges were jealous of it. The lord must produce a royal grant to justify his action; and if the grant was not perfectly in order, if for example the King's seal on it had been damaged, the lord would pay a heavy fine and lose his right of justice forever. Edward I in particular disliked these private criminal courts, and a sensible lord would rather keep the good will of the King than stand up for the letter of his rights.

King Edward I did not tamper with the legal right of the manor court to bring back a fugitive serf; such a fundamental alteration in the law of the land could only be carried into effect by the unanimous consent of his barons. But by administrative regulation he made the right worthless. Beyond the bounds of the manor the manor court had no power of arrest, and the King's courts would not enforce its judgments. The lord might threaten terrible penalties against his fugitive serf, and of course he confiscated anything the runaway had left behind; but unless the serf was so foolish as to come back

102

within the bounds of the manor nothing could be done to him.

What really governed the life of the peasant was the custom of his manor, and these customs were infinitely various. There seems to be no reason behind their variations, no underlying rule that for very fertile land the tenant must do more work on the demesne than for poor land. A possible explanation is that the juries who answered questions put to them by the Domesday Book commissioners did not everywhere take the same view of their duty. They were on oath, and probably they wanted to tell the truth; but in some places they related exactly what their Saxon lords had made them do, and in others they said what a just lord would make them do. For whatever reason, the answers differed widely.

It is time now to come to our concrete example, remembering all the time that there were other peasants in England either better or worse off, and that our peasant is not so typical as the Earl or the country knight.

Tom Hill holds a plowland in the manor of Stretton St. Thomas. He lives in the village of Stretton, which is divided between the two manors of Stretton St. Thomas and Stretton Braose. Sometimes we suppose that every manor was a village and the other way around, but by the thirteenth century, after the original large holdings of the Conquest had been cut up by two centuries of marriage portions and allotments to younger sons, the divided village was not uncommon. Tom's wife is named Margaret, and they have three children of the same names and ages as those described in the earlier chapters. Once again it is the dawn of a fine August day.

At first light the family wake, and waste little time in dressing. Their home is a cottage of two rooms, of which only one is intended for human occupation; the other, at the back, houses the two oxen which are the chief wealth of the household. Their single room has few furnishings. The floor is of beaten earth, the walls of whitewashed clay supported on a timber frame, the roof of thatch held up by timber crucks. These crucks are about twelve feet apart, the length of an average rafter, and the roof is formed by eight pairs of them. That makes it twice the size of the poorest huts in the village, which have only eight crucks apiece. Such cottages are not expected to last long, but they are easily replaced. When Tom Hill built this one, ten years ago, he had only to beg timber crucks from the lord, and ask his neighbors to help him raise them; the thatch of the roof and the clay walls he put in place singlehanded.

The children sleep on a pile of straw on the floor; their parents have a straw mattress raised on posts above the draft which sweeps under the ill-fitting door. There is a smoke hole in the roof, directly above the flat stone which serves as a hearth; but for the sake of extra warmth there are no windows in the walls. When Tom gets up the first thing he does is to open the top half of the door to let in light and ventilation.

Perhaps the only things in the cottage which have a definite money value are the iron cooking pot and its trivet and chain, worth eight pence in all. There are also a few wooden platters and horn mugs, but these are so easily made at home that they are not listed in the inventories of peasant households which have come down to us. No family can live without at least one cooking pot, but today there is no fire on the hearth. Fuel is too scarce to be squandered on fires in summer. Margaret cooks once a week, on Sundays.

The family have slept in their clothes, with their mantles for coverlet. Tom and the boys wear shirts and tunics, of unbleached wool brown with dirt, and long leggings which end at the ankle; Anne and her mother wear smocks and kirtles. In August all go barefoot; though for the mud and snow of winter they have leg-bandages like puttees, and shoes which are shapeless bags of cowhide with the hair left on. When they get up they tie on girdles of grass rope, so that a woman may adjust the length of her kirtle and a man make a handy pocket in the upper part of his tunic.

Anne and her mother bundle up their hair under tattered kerchiefs. Tom and the boys have each a broad-brimmed straw hat, which they have woven for themselves. In very cold weather they keep their ears warm under coifs made of thick cloth, and put up the hoods attached to their mantles of rough frieze.

Nobody washes face or hands. Water has to be fetched from the spring in a wooden bucket, and is used sparingly. Besides, they are accustomed to being always dirty and smelly, like all their friends. They have no soap and no towels. Cleanliness is a badge of the gentry, and a peasant who washed himself every day would be considered odd and uppish, trying to give himself airs. After each member of the family has drunk a mug of ale and swallowed a small lump of rye bread they are ready for the day.

The parish church of Stretton, like one of the two manors, belongs to the abbey of St. Thomas. That is to say, the monks take the tithe and the offerings on condition they put in a vicar to say Mass. This village is luckier than some other vicarages; the conscientious abbot has found a vicar who is an ordained priest, willing to perform the duties for which he is paid. Mass is offered daily in the parish church at sunrise. All five of the Hill family attend regularly; today they go there as soon as they have finished their breakfast.

Because they have broken their fast they cannot receive Communion. But laymen who received Communion every day would have been considered very eccentric. They communicate only at Christmas and Easter. One reason for this is that the vicar dislikes hearing confessions; he is paid a very small wage to say a daily Mass and grumbles if his parochial duties take up any more of his time. Once every six months he consents to spend the morning in the confessional; he is always willing to anoint the dying or to conduct a wedding or baptism or funeral, but for these extra services he expects a fee.

The church is fairly full, because pious laymen have come from two neighboring parishes. In one of these no Mass has been offered in the church for the last two years. The rector, who is himself only a deacon and so cannot say Mass, is studying at Oxford where he will remain for

many years to come. The Bishop could not refuse him permission to complete his education and so fit himself for the priesthood; it is one of the recognized excuses for absence from a benefice. Of course the missing rector ought to provide a competent vicar, and before he left for Oxford he promised the Bishop that he would do so. If he neglects his promise long enough the Bishop will take some action; but the rector is a younger son of a powerful and influential baronial family, and a delay of a mere two years is not grave enough to merit starting a feud in the diocese.

The other neighboring parish is also deprived of a regular Mass. The vicar there is both lazy and greedy; he has taken over another church some miles away for the sake of the double stipend, and neglects each one with the excuse that he is busy in the other.

Every responsible churchman agrees that the system of absentee rectors and negligent vicars causes grave scandal. The trouble is that it has already been remedied, in theory; but there is no one with the energy and the spare time to see that the excellent regulations are carried into effect. Church councils have laid down that every incumbent must be in priest's orders and enjoy a clear income of at least five pounds a year; but if a starving clerk is willing to accept a lesser stipend, if a deacon explains that he is only waiting for his bishop to find time to ordain him, busy men with other and more important duties than the enforcement of these regulations are inclined to let things slide. A suit in the Bishop's court would cause bad feeling in the parish; if the unsatisfactory vicar is removed the church may be for years without any incumbent; rectors should be encouraged to attend the University and they are entitled to leave of absence while completing their studies. Above all, some clerks enjoy the friendship and backing of the King, and others have powerful influence at Rome. Everyone admits that in this fallen world such people may laugh at the law.

The parishioners of Stretton are comparatively well off. Their vicar is ignorant and poor, but he does his duty according to his lights. Their tithes go to an abbey forty miles away, whose monks would never demean themselves by taking parish duty. But at least their rector does not live in Rome or some other foreign country, and an abbey acknowledges the obligation of alms-giving. There is no prosperous rectory where a man down on his luck may ask for temporary assistance, but if famine were to strike the whole parish the villagers would be kept from starvation if they walked forty miles to beg at the abbey door.

The vicar is one of themselves, which makes for friendliness. He speaks their dialect and understands their problems. His lack of education means that he will never gain preferment, and he likes to keep on good terms with the flock among whom he will end his life. He is, as a matter of fact, Tom Hill's second cousin; but then Tom Hill has cousins in many different stations of life. That is one of the advantages of living in exactly the same place as his great-great-grandfather.

Today, as is customary, Roger Hill serves the Mass. He has learned the responses parrot fashion, for he understands very little Latin. But the vicar is beginning to teach him the daily prayers, and how to read them from a clumsy hornbook. This is a folded tablet of wood, with the Our Father scratched on one side and the Hail Mary on the other; the writing on the wooden pages is protected from dirty hands by a transparent covering of horn.

Whenever the vicar goes out, to take Viaticum to the sick, to bury the dead, or to baptize a new parishioner, Roger goes with him and watches carefully. He is learning the priestly office by the direct method of apprenticeship. He cannot be taught in this way to hear confessions, since all that passes in the confessional is secret; but he knows how the poor live, and what are their temptations, which will make him more useful as a village priest than many a scholar and gentleman.

Roger hopes to become a priest, and the hope is not absurd. There is a legal obstacle. He is a serf, and no serf may be ordained. But his monastic lords will not obstruct the career of a young man who wishes to serve God; if the Bishop is willing to ordain him the abbot is certain to grant him his freedom. That particular law, which seems to us so queer and unchristian, was designed to prevent two different scandals: a priest who is the servant of a layman cannot freely fulfill his ministry; a village may be denuded of essential workers if too many peasants enter the priesthood merely to live without hard manual work.

Meanwhile Roger is diligently learning all that the vicar can teach him, which is not a great deal: reading and writing, and a little elementary Latin. He pays for his lessons by personal service; the Hill family hardly ever pay in ready money for anything. He cleans floors and runs errands, and accompanies the vicar on all his visits, ringing a little bell to warn passers-by to kneel if the Sacrament is being carried to the sick. Since he eats and sleeps at home he costs the vicar nothing.

That gives Roger a much easier life than the usual alternative: that he should be boarded and lodged by the priest in return for his services. The average village priest was desperately poor, and the priest's boy proverbially the poorest creature in the parish; so that to cheat him in any way was as despicable as to steal pennies from a blind beggar.

Freed from the burden of keeping a servant the vicar is as well off with his five pounds a year as most of his parishioners. Some of them earn more, but he has no family to support. He is grateful to Roger, and will recommend him to the Bishop when he applies for ordination. The Bishop is entirely dependent on these personal recommendations; there are no seminaries or theological colleges where a candidate's character may be tested before ordination.

If all goes well and Roger becomes a priest, he expects to hold a vicarage in some village, perhaps his own village of Stretton, until he dies. His meager education will prevent him from climbing higher, since he is not outstanding either for brains or holiness. All the same, for the poor boy of genuine ability the Church provides a career open to talent. The only Englishman to become Pope, more than a century before the period of this book, was the son of a poor peasant attached to the Abbey of St. Albans. In the higher reaches of the royal administration there are always a few bishops and clerks of such obscure origin that their enemies may plausibly reproach them with servile birth.

After Mass, Roger puts out the candles and washes the cruets, and then stays behind in the church with the vicar, to continue his construing from the big missal on the altar. The missal is the only book in the village, and not every country parish church owns a complete copy. But the monks who enjoy the profits of the rectory are conscientious men who equip their church properly.

The other members of the family go off to work in the fields, which is how they pass all the hours of daylight except on Sundays and other holidays. Tom Hill yokes his oxen and leads them off to the demesne. August is one of the few months when no plowing is done, but there is an aftermath of hay to be carted to the ricks, and when that is finished the bailiff will find some other work for him. Margaret, Ralph, and Anne go to work on their own holding.

Tom Hill's yoke of oxen make him a man of some importance in the working of the manor. They are one-sixth of a full plow team; though nowadays, in fine weather at least, plows are often drawn by lesser teams of eight or ten beasts. For carting hay, in the small carts of those days, his yoke will make a full team and he will drive them by himself, on his own responsibility. For the plowing of the demesne the bailiff makes up teams from the oxen of several peasants, but when it comes to plowing his own land Tom must himself come to an arrangement with his neighbors. In the agriculture of the thirteenth century there was a great deal of plowing to be done. After harvest, as soon as the stubble had been grazed, the land was broken up, and kept under plow through the winter until next year's grain began to germinate. There was no other way of keeping down the weeds.

The law would maintain that these oxen belong, not to Tom, but to the abbey which in theory owns all he possesses. But only a very ruthless tyrant would enforce that outdated law. If Tom wishes he may sell his oxen, as a few years ago after an exceptionally good harvest he bought them. But when he dies and Ralph inherits the holding, the bailiff will select for the abbey the best of his beasts. That is the heriot, a primitive form of death duty; it corresponds to the relief paid by an heir in a higher station of life.

Tom does not expect to live long. He is just forty, but already he is sometimes reckoned an old man. He is out in all weathers, and often wet; in winter he is usually cold as well. He walks clumsily and slowly because of his rheumatism; and his bare feet, though hard and horny, always have a few cuts on them. Sometimes he feels ill; but the land must be cultivated and he cannot easily take to his bed. The first serious disease he catches will kill him. There is no doctor within reach, and if there was a doctor his remedies would be more lethal than any sickness.

But when Tom comes to die (with the consolations of religion and perhaps the prayers of a son in the priesthood) Ralph will succeed him with the same rights and duties and perhaps rather more wealth than his father. Tom will have been useful on earth, and he will leave his family secure. No man can hope for more.

In Stretton he is a person of importance, even though he is still a serf. One reason for this is that though the village has been divided between two manors the King still sees it as a unit. Twice a year the able-bodied men of the village journey to the hundred court—the local court of the county division—where the King's sheriff reads out to them any writs about police matters and the preservation of order which have reached him from the central government. The single village, not the two manors, elects a constable to keep the peace, and reports to the King's coroner the finding of unexplained corpses. The sheriff, not the lords of the manors, holds the view of frankpledge, checking that every man is a member of a group of ten who will be jointly responsible if any one of them should happen to break the law. Tom is a tithing-man, the spokesman of his group. It is not an arduous post. The peasants do not regard the view of frankpledge very seriously, though in earlier times it was a useful method of keeping order. Among themselves they call it "the trimming," because the sheriff seems more eager to inflict petty fines on those who are not in the correct tithing than to enforce collective responsibility.

The monks would be seriously annoyed if their serfs, who are needed on the land, were called away for military service; lawyers will tell you that a serf should not use or even possess arms. But Tom keeps in the thatch of his cottage a well-greased iron spearhead, which can easily be fixed to the handle of a hoe if the villagers think it feasible to defend themselves against robbers. If the constable should blow his horn, as a warning that a fugitive from justice is crossing the land of the village, it will be Tom's duty to join in the hue and cry, at least until the outlaw has been pursued to the next village. The villagers will not chase him too fast, for if they caught him they would have to waste time attending his trial when they ought to be working on the land, besides the danger of getting mixed up in a blood-feud with the fugitive's kin if he is hanged; but they must see that he keeps moving, or the sheriff will fine them.

Tom has never actually used a weapon; though in his youth he once stood with the other men of the village, defying three stragglers from a baronial army until the rascals rode away to plunder an easier prey. He would do it again if he had to.

It is bad luck that such a pillar of the community should still be a serf, especially now that most of his cousins who work on the other manor have bought their freedom. The trouble is that the cellarer of the abbey, the man who controls its finances, has scruples about diminishing the resources which one day he must hand on to his successor; if a serf buys his freedom the abbey profits by a lump sum, but future monks will have lost a servant. The cellarer has not yet been persuaded to sell freedom to any of his serfs.

There are compensations; in some ways an abbey is a better lord than a lay noble. The community never dies, and therefore is never called on suddenly to pay an enormous relief to the King. The abbey pays taxes, of course, to both Pope and King; in general a wealthy religious house pays more in taxation than a lay baron. But the tax can be foreseen, and there is no great urgency about paying it. The obedientiary who comes down every Michaelmas to collect the profits of the manor is never in such desperate straits for money as the steward of a lay lord. Above all, monks are obliged by their profession to be charitable. It is never absurd, and sometimes profitable, to appeal to their generosity.

But in good years, and this is a good year, the cellarer stands on the letter of his rights; he dare not be generous with the income of his community. So that even at this slack season of the year serfs must put in every hour of their weekly labor. Tom Hill and his oxen plod off fairly happily to the demesne, knowing that no very hard work awaits them.

As rent for his holding Tom pays a silver penny at Christmas and another at Whitsun; which is in itself a contradiction, since in strict law any money a serf may acquire belongs of right to his lord. But these petty payments are rather an acknowledgment of lordship than an economic rent. What the bailiff values is the labor service of the tenants.

On this manor every holding owes three days' work a week; with extra days at haysel—the haying season—

harvest, and sowing, as many as are needed to get the job finished. That sounds as though Tom worked more than half his time on the lord's demesne, and would seldom be free to cultivate his own holding. But it is not so bad as it sounds.

A holding owes the work of one man only. At present Tom must go in person, but within a few years he will be able to send Ralph in his stead. Margaret and her children are working on the holding today, and among them they can do more than a single man. By custom the "day's work" ends at dinnertime, leaving the afternoon free. For the extra days at periods of special pressure he must work until sunset, but the bailiff must give him his dinner. At harvesttime the whole village turns out to reap, from toddlers to old women; for until the harvest has been gathered no one can be sure of food for the winter. We do well to remember that even at the present day there is never two years' food stored up anywhere for the whole world; though if our local harvest should fail we may import grain from far away. In the 1270s the fields of Stretton must feed the people of Stretton, and leave something over for their lords. If the local harvest is insufficient they will starve, since they have no money to buy grain from abroad; if they had the money, heavy wagons loaded with grain cannot travel far over the rutted roads.

The recurring days of work every week are known as weekworks, and the extra days at times of special pressure as *beneficia,* or in English as beneworks. The modern

117

beanfeast, or beano, still given by some old-fashioned English firms to their workpeople, is really the bene feast, held at the end of the harvest benework.

Meanwhile Ralph and Anne and their mother are busy on the family holding, though I am not at all sure what they would have been doing at the beginning of August: clearing drains, perhaps, or furbishing their iron sickles in readiness for the harvest which will begin in a few days. Margaret may be showing her daughter how to gather the cut grain into a shock and tie it with a rope of straw made on the spot. In the harvest field the women go behind the men, stacking and binding the grain as it is reaped; behind them again come the veterans and toddlers, gleaning any ears that have been missed. The men try to reap faster than their womenfolk can gather, and the girls try to shame the young men by standing with empty hands waiting for more grain to be cut.

Even in these last days before harvest there is more to be done on the land than looking after the grain; though grain, chiefly rye and barley with a little wheat on the best land, is by far the most important and valuable product of the farming year. The Hills own a cow and thirty ewes, whose milking is the task of the women. In the whole village there are only one bull and one ram, in the care of the vicar. The council of village elders chose the animals in the first place. The vicar, who does not plow all day, is the obvious man to take charge of them.

The rector, by the way, holds a glebe of two plowlands, the endowment given five hundred years ago by the Saxon thane who held land of the king and set up the parish.

But with the other profits of the rectory these plowlands now belong to the abbey and are worked with the demesne, so that only their title deeds show that they are church land. One day the King will try to tax this glebe, and when the abbey claims exemption for it as church land there will be a splendid lawsuit, enough to keep a jury busy for months.

At midmorning everyone stops work for a snack. The Hills have brought bread and cheese in an old kerchief, and a little leather bottle of ale. Tom is sitting under a tree with the other workers on the demesne, while his family have their special shady spot on their own land. Soon after midday work stops on the demesne. Tom leads his oxen back to his cottage, where he meets his wife and children.

They still have plenty of bread, even during these August days just before harvest; last year was a good one. Sometimes the crop does not quite last out the year, and then everyone must manage on nettles and stored acorns for a week or so until the new harvest has been reaped. It is luckily easier to live hungry in the warmest season of the year.

In summer no prudent housewife wastes fuel in cooking. The village is always short of firewood. The villagers are entitled to take furze and scrub from the waste, though they may not cut timber without special leave from the lord. In one particular coppice they have the right to cut branches "by hook or by crook," provided they do not kill the growing tree trunks; the privilege, said to be founded on a very ancient and now lost charter,

119

must have been granted by some charitable lord, so long ago that his name has been forgotten and no one now remembers to pray for his soul.

But in most of the forest the "vert," the growing greenery, is as strictly preserved as the venison. The King is jealous of his hunting, and thick undergrowth is needed to provide cover for his game. In these parts there is no peat, and the sedge by the stream is needed for fodder in hard winters.

With woodland all around them, woodland which has grown without human agency, the villagers are often hard put to it to make a fire in frosty weather. They are convinced that the forest ought to be free to all—not seeing that if this were so there would soon be no forest left. The tradition has been handed down from their forefathers that it is all the fault of William the Conqueror and his newfangled Forest Law, though in truth forest laws of a sort were at least as old as King Canute. This is one of the most bitterly resented rules of the medieval economy; every man of spirit raids the forest for firewood whenever he can do it without being caught. If he should happen to be caught he faces a severe penalty, a year's imprisonment for the first offense. But if the King were to imprison an able-bodied man for a whole year he would have to pay for his keep, and perhaps a holding of land would go uncultivated. The royal foresters prefer to allow the individual culprit to escape, and then levy a collective fine on his village to make good the estimated damage.

Even with the aid of stolen brushwood fuel is still

scarce, and today the Hills will eat a cold dinner. Since they are without tables or chairs they squat on the earthen floor of the cottage while Margaret takes hunks of black bread from a wooden shelf in the corner. Everyone has a knife. But there is a feeling against cutting bread with iron, a feeling hardly strong enough to be called a superstition. They prefer to pull the loaves to pieces with their hands.

Besides bread they have milk and cheese, though rather as seasoning, to be eaten sparingly, than as solid food. Tom and Ralph, the able-bodied men, receive also a morsel of bacon; but meat is too precious to be given to women and children. This prosperous family eats no greenstuff; though in some cottages their poorer neighbors are filling up empty corners with cold cabbage cooked last Sunday.

Meanwhile Tom grumbles about the other great grievance which afflicts all peasants, second only to the appropriation of the forest which should be free to all. He feels sure that this bread was never made from their own excellent rye; and the flour has been badly ground. The miller has been up to his tricks again.

The miller whose wheel is turned by the village stream (windmills are very rare) has a monopoly; or rather, the lord has the monopoly and rents it at a stiff price to the miller. All grain grown on the manor must be ground at the manor mill, and the miller takes payment by keeping back a proportion. The trouble is that the miller alone measures the grain, with no one to check his measurements. It is common gossip that he and his family eat finer flour than any of his customers; and they always have enough, even in the hardest seasons. Besides, he does not understand his job nearly so well as the miller in the next village. But nothing can be done about it. If the whole village were to complain to the abbot he might get rid of this particular miller. But the man who would come to take his place might not be an improvement, and all the peasants would be haunted by the knowledge that they had done a fellow peasant out of a good job. Tom finishes his grumble by quoting the old saying: There are a few honest millers in the world—you can spot one by the tuft of hair growing out of the palm of his hand.

Everyone eats a lot, and feels grateful for it. It is not impossible that they will be hungry by next spring; but it is a waste of time to calculate further than the remains of the harvest now stored in the village barns. Then they go out again to work; a midday nap would squander precious daylight.

Tom leads his whole family to the edge of the waste, to continue work on a project which will bring them great benefits if they can carry it out before winter. With the permission of the lord and the village council Tom has fenced in an acre on the verge of the waste, and herded his pigs there all summer. The pigs have rooted out the scrub; of course no sizable trees grew in that acre or he would not have been allowed to fence it in the first place. Now, with the aid of his family, he hopes to grub up the last roots before harvesting begins. In the winter he will snatch an hour or two to plow it, and in the spring sow rye. By next year he will have a patch of ground which he may cultivate as he likes. He may grow on it saffron, or carrots, or medicinal herbs. That was the great advantage of these patches won from the waste, known as assarts.

On his holding in the common fields Tom Hill must work with the other villagers. Plowing and harvesting must be communal affairs, since no villager can make up a full team from his own oxen; if a lazy neighbor will not weed his strip the whole field suffers, unless someone else is public-spirited enough to weed it for him. If the village council should guess wrong about the weather, and start the harvest at the wrong time, the whole community will feel it. Except for spreading lime or dung on his land, a competent and industrious peasant cannot do anything that will make his holding more fruitful than that of the village wastrel. On an assart he is his own master.

Of course he will pay a rent in money to his lord, the monks who own the waste as well as the fields of the manor. That is another legal contradiction, a serf paying rent in money. But in the village, serfdom is regarded as an unimportant disability which afflicts especially the tenants of ecclesiastical lords. Nearly all the tenants on the other manor are personally free; but freemen and serfs argue on terms of equality in the village council, and their sons and daughters intermarry. There happens to be one freeman in the manor of Stretton St. Thomas; or rather, he is a freeman outside the manor and a serf within it. John Brown wandered in from somewhere else

123

during the bad times of the Montfort War. Though he was free he took over a servile holding, and does labor service for it like the rest of them. Lawyers call him a "serf regardant," a serf in his dealings with the abbey and a free man in his dealings with the sheriff; though only a lawyer could remember such a complicated status. John Brown will be a foreigner in the village until he dies of old age, but he married a local girl and his children are accepted as members of the community.

Tom's holding in the village fields must descend to young Ralph. Tom himself cannot dispose of it. But the assart he may leave, if he wishes, to Roger or Anne, or to some religious house in return for prayers for his soul. If he needs money urgently he may sell it, though only to a purchaser approved by the lord. It is his.

Every energetic peasant in Stretton is assarting as much land as his family can clear. The monks do not refuse permission, since it brings more land under cultivation and makes the village more productive. But they are growing a little worried at the shrinkage of the waste, which is needed for so many purposes. One day they will have to call a halt, unless the village begins to dwindle of its own accord. They are sure that will happen before a crisis is reached. They cannot imagine that England as a whole has an expanding population; they have been brought up in a static world.

Work stops in time for everyone to be home by sunset. The Hills squat on the floor of their cottage for another light meal of bread and milk. Afterward they do not go straight to sleep, as they would in winter. This is the peak of the year, with harvest in prospect; they want to meet their neighbors and lay plans for the future.

Next Sunday at Mass the vicar will consecrate the Lammas loaf, and on Monday reaping will begin. Two days ago the wheat for the Lammas loaf was reaped in a sunny corner of the demesne. It was not really ripe, but the miller managed to turn it into some sort of flour, and the baker lit his oven specially on a weekday to bake it. There is only just enough of it for the priest's Communion; but then the villagers never take Communion in August, or at any other time save Christmas and Easter.

The first Sunday in August is really too early to bake even a small loaf from the grain of the new harvest; but the villagers have done it since their ancestors became Christian more than five hundred years ago. Perhaps in those days the climate was warmer.

Lammas, the Loaf Mass, is an achievement. There has actually been a harvest, even though a very small one; which proves that there will be food for the coming winter. As a matter of fact this year's harvest promises to be plentiful; there will be plenty to drink as well as plenty to eat.

In Stretton they grow rye, barley, oats, and wheat, which can all be made into bread if famine threatens. In normal years the wheat is sold on the market, to provide expensive white bread for the gentry; oats are eaten by the animals, or sold as fodder for knightly destriers; rye furnishes the daily bread of the villagers; and the barley is brewed into ale.

In the village there is only one baker, another result of the perpetual fuel shortage; though it is said that in the North, where peat is plentiful, every housewife has her own baking oven.

The baker does not himself knead all the dough eaten in the village. His chief duty is to provide a hot oven, where Margaret and the other housewives may bake their own flour, paying for it by letting him keep a proportion. He bakes for a few widowers who have no one to cook for them, and as his oven cools he also cooks the rare joints of beef or mutton that are eaten in the village.

Brewing is done by the housewives, without professional help. There are no hops in the ale, and therefore it turns sour after a few days. Margaret brews once a fortnight, with a group of other village women who club together to contribute fuel. It is very good news that all the barley of this good harvest may be brewed, instead of being wasted on bread.

After supper Tom Hill goes off to the village council, to discuss the final arrangements for the reaping. Margaret visits the baker, where other women will be gossiping about the Lammas feast. Ralph and Anne go courting.

In that aspect of their lives they are better off than the gentry. No grownup will arrange a marriage for them. They are free to choose for themselves.

In practice the choice is limited. In a village of two hundred souls there will not be many bachelors or unmarried girls. Peasants from the neighborhood may be met at Stretton Church, but since the abbey maintains only a grange, not a manor house, there is no staff of idle servingmen and maids to spend more time in love-making than honest plowmen can afford. The other manor on the far side of the village is not the main residence of its lord, and usually lies empty. Anne, who is planning to marry the man of her choice in about three years' time, had a dozen to choose from among her contemporaries and playmates. Ralph chose from an even more limited field. He has picked a sturdy, plain, even-tempered girl who can cook and wash clothes by beating them against a flat stone. He is not passionately in love with her, but she will manage his house well.

Anne's young man has been free for some years, since his father bought the freedom of his whole family from the secular manorial lord. When she marries she herself will be reckoned free, and her children after her; though here or there you might find a lawyer who still holds to the old maxim of Roman law that a servile mother must bear servile children whatever the condition of the father. Ralph's children will be serfs, until some improvident or forward-looking abbot can be persuaded to sell freedom to all the serfs on his manor. That will make no difference socially, and very little difference in law unless one of the villagers gets himself mixed up in a serious case before the King's judges.

Besides courting, the young people are planning the festivities for Lammas afternoon. Though peasants work hard the Church provides them with generous holidays:

about eighty days in the year, counting Sundays and holy days and the longer breaks at Christmas and Easter. We have enjoyed these holidays for so many generations that we are inclined to take them for granted, forgetting that in many parts of the world people normally work a seven-day week. In the morning there will be the Loaf Mass, and at midday the almost equally serious function of dinner. In the afternoon the villagers will enjoy themselves.

The basic amusement is the dance, a public communal dance in which all the young women twirl in a ring while the young men dance in a larger ring outside. There is no choosing of partners, and the exercise has no connection with love-making. Long ago, when their ancestors first danced it, they were making magic to persuade the seasons to recur in due order. That is now forgotten, but the dance is still taken seriously. These peasants try to dance well, as soldiers try to drill well, because it is an important activity which ought to be well done. They will try very hard, and anyone who makes a false step must apologize humbly. The music will be a bagpipe.

Besides dancing there will be various contests in which the young men may display their vigor; but for magical reasons that have now been forgotten these contests occur more often in the spring than at harvesttime. On Shrove Tuesday the two manors compete in a long, savage, scattered game of football. The goals are more than a mile apart, and the only rule seriously enforced is that forbidding the use of deadly weapons. The ball is the inflated bladder of a pig. At Pentecost there is a rather cruel competition, in which the men throw sticks at a cock

129

dangling by the legs from a high pole; the man who kills the cock keeps it for his supper. On St. John's Eve, at midsummer, the young people jump over bonfires. But there is no particular magic or good luck about Lammas; the bringing in of the Corn Dolly—a human image made from the last sheaf, probably once an emblem of a pagan corn god—and the other rejoicings which teach the grain to grow will be carried through at harvest home about Michaelmas. On this afternoon of Lammas the young men will run races, compete in high jump and broad jump, perhaps wrestle; there will be no feeling that such-and-such must be done, to bring good luck to the fields. Luck has already done its work, as the existence of the Loaf Mass proves. They will enjoy themselves because it is a holiday, and for no stronger reason.

Everyone will drink rather too much ale, and perhaps the Hill family will dine on a leg of tough old ewe mutton. Three or four times a year they eat meat, as befits a prosperous household.

There will be no archery. We think of the longbow as characteristic of medieval England; actually it was a development of the fourteenth century or later. At this time the bow is a Welsh weapon, little known among true Englishmen.

The Hills are on the whole a happy family. Tom worries in the spring, when he is sowing his grain; Margaret worries in late summer, for fear that the flour will not last until harvest; Roger has chosen a disciplined life, and sometimes wonders whether he will have the fortitude to go through with it. But when at last he is vicar of Stretton he will be an important figure in the village, and with so many cousins at hand he will never feel lonely in his bachelorhood. Ralph and Anne are enjoying the happiest time of their lives, though they may not know it. They do not have to worry about dependents, and if food should run short they are hardy enough to manage on short rations. They are content in their illiteracy, and pity poor Roger who must work so hard at that difficult business of reading and writing. The village is their home, quite big enough to make a fascinating world. They have no wish to leave it, and they will not.

Lordship is accepted, by both serfs and freemen. Peasants grumble about working on the demesne, especially when their own holdings need attention. But private ownership of land is the basis of their lives, and if the lord's title were impugned their own acres would be insecure. The lord still gives protection in return for service, as old men can remember from the days of civil war. Every year there are a few more mouths to be fed, but there is waste land waiting for the plow and plenty of strong hands to clear it. They themselves produce nearly everything they eat or wear or use. In the affairs of daily life they rarely need money, and the few pennies they must pay annually are easily got by selling a pig or a sheep or a few bushels of grain in the market.

A hundred years later peasants will burn granges and destroy manorial records throughout England, with a special hatred against monastic lords. But that will come after the shock of the Black Death, shock enough to make a simple man question all the foundations of his life; and especially after the lords, in their Parliament, have altered the rules in the middle of the game just because the shortage of peasants seems to promise the survivors the chance of a better life. Agrarian discontent lingered on until the land enclosures of the eighteenth century destroyed the peasantry and left nothing but rich farmers and landless laborers; but in the 1270s it had not yet arisen.

# IV

## THE FAMILY OF A RICH MERCHANT

Though John White is one of the most eminent merchants of London the outside of his house is nothing remarkable. From the street a passer-by sees only a few yards of high stone wall, broken in the middle by tall wooden double gates. It is half an hour before sunrise on a fine August morning, and as the watchman proclaims the end of curfew and the bells of a hundred parish churches ring for early Mass a wicket set in the great gate is unbarred and women come out with buckets to draw water from the conduit nearby. A few minutes later the great gates are opened and a string of laden packponies emerge. They have been loaded by lantern light for an

133

early start, but they cannot leave London before the city gates open at sunrise. During the night all London concentrates on security and self-defense. The watch will question anyone found in the street and take him to the lockup if he cannot give a good account of himself; no one may enter or leave the city; houses are securely bolted and barred, and if a messenger should bang on the gate he will be questioned through a loophole before he is admitted. London is a very great and rich city; but it has absolutely no night life, either for business or pleasure.

Now, as the gates are thrown open, we can see that the headquarters of this great business establishment are larger than they seem from the outside. The mesnage runs back a long way. Mesnage is the legal term for a house with its courts and other appurtenances; at some time between the thirteenth and the twentieth centuries some conveyancer misread a manuscript N for U, and the queer word *messuage* got into our modern title deeds.

London houses were originally built upon long plots, running back from a narrow frontage on the street. The first settlers in Saxon London could not earn their living solely by trade or craftsmanship; so that behind every house which faced the street lay a considerable garden, almost a smallholding, which they might cultivate in their spare time. Down through the years many of these long narrow plots have been cut up into courts, with little houses crowding around them; but John White owns an undivided mesnage.

Within its double gates lies a cobbled forecourt, just large enough for a wagon to turn around. Behind this rises the gable end of the house proper, with the front door at ground level, a window above it, and within the slope of the gabled roof another door beside a windlass, for hoisting goods to the storeroom in the attic. The long narrow house is placed to one side of the plot to leave room for the alley, wide enough for wheeled traffic, which leads to the main warehouse at the far end of the back yard. Stabling occupies the lower floor of the warehouse; in the back yard stand a few isolated sheds, the privy, the coal-store, the kitchen (isolated as a precaution against fire), the well, which is surrounded with a high curb to keep out rubbish but whose water is so foul all the same that it can be drunk only by animals. At the far end the plot is divided by a stone wall from the back of a similar plot facing another street; the sides also are bounded by stone walls, put in a few years ago at the request of the city authorities to replace the timber palisades which used to spread accidental fires throughout the town.

Fire is the most dangerous enemy of crowded London. Sparks rise constantly from the many smoke holes and rare chimneys to land on a neighbor's roof. The city regulations have banned thatch in favor of tiles, but for two opposite reasons these regulations are difficult to enforce. Some Londoners are too poor to roof their little hovels with expensive tile; others are so prominent and powerful that no one can compel them to obey the law.

When a timber-framed house catches fire it will inevitably burn to the ground; without pressure pumps there is no way to save it. Neighbors may carry water in buckets, to keep the flames at bay while life and property are saved; the city authorities concentrate on stopping the fire from spreading. Among the common possessions of every ward are long poles, ending in stout metal hooks. These may be used to pull down burning thatch before a house is thoroughly alight; or they can be thrust through the doorway of a cottage and hooked into a beam of the opposite wall. Then two or three strong men push sideways, using the doorpost as fulcrum to the lever, until the far wall collapses and the cottage lies level with the ground. That is the easiest way to clear a firebreak around a burning house; the owner of the wrecked cottage will not complain very strongly, for if his little house had not been pulled down it would undoubtedly have burned to the ground.

After the last burning of the White family's house, fifty years ago, John White's father rebuilt it mainly in stone. The roof is covered in red clay tiles. Smoke from the hearth is led up a tall stone chimney, which catches most of the sparks before they can get out. With no thatch anywhere and stone walls around the plot, John White can expect his splendid mansion to endure for many years.

It is indeed a splendid mansion, one of the finest in London. The whole ground floor is one big hall; in the middle rises the chimney, going up through the floor above and warming the whole house with the coals which smolder on the stone hearth day and night. Coal has recently become a common fuel in London, where firewood rose in price as the nearer coppices were cut down. It is carried by sea from the Tyne; colliers (coal ships) form a substantial proportion of the traffic in the Pool of London, and the city administration has already passed ordinances against excessive smoke.

The hall is stone-built throughout: floor of stone flags, walls of stone rubble between ashlar facings, unglazed lancet windows within stone frames. At each end stands a large timber door. The inner surface of the walls has been covered with a thin coating of plaster, on which a recurring pattern has been painted through a stencil. The whole effect is rich and civilized, though a little gloomy. Only above does it seem uncouth; for the town house of several stories is a new development and no one has found out a satisfactory treatment for its divisions. There is no ceiling, so that you see over your head plain undecorated joists and planks, with light showing through the cracks. This woodwork was originally stained brown, but it has been blackened by smoke from the torches set in rings against the wall.

In one corner a flight of stone stairs leads to the second floor. Here masonry ends, and the walls are of plaster framed in timber. The unglazed wooden window frames are barred by vertical wooden rods, square in section and set corner to corner: an ingenious dodge to let in as much light as possible while keeping out the hands of thieves.

Above lies a third floor, whose walls are the slopes of the roof, so that only in the middle may a man stand upright. It is lit by windows in the gable ends. Since nothing but tiles keep out the weather it is hot in summer and cold in winter. It is not normally lived in, but used for storage.

On the second floor are the family living quarters. Parlor, solar, and best bedchamber are walled off by permanent planking, and the remaining space is divided into cubicles by movable lattices. At this level the stairs end. The only access to the attic is by a ladder fixed to the wall; heavy stores are hoisted by the windlass at the gable end.

The Whites are just getting up to face the day. John White and his wife Joan have just left their great bed, which stands against a blank wall, guarded from drafts by curtains and a flat canopy. It is a very large and comfortable bed, with a feather mattress enclosed in linen and feather pillows cased in silk; over the fine woolen blankets lies a silk coverlet.

The chamber as a whole is more comfortable than any apartment in the Earl's great castle. The floor is covered deep in fresh sweet hay; besides the usual chest at the foot of the bed there is a table against the wall bearing a mirror of polished steel and an ivory casket for trinkets; instead of smoky torches a lamp burns scented oil. Master and lady have the room to themselves; in this narrow crowded house there is no need for a servant to sleep beside them in a trundle bed. The fact is that John White is nearly as rich as the Earl, but does not have to spend his money on retainers and fortifications. He buys comfort instead of power.

In other rooms on the same floor sleep his children,

with the same names and ages as the others in this book. Ralph and Roger share a bed nearly as splendid as their parents'. They have just got out of it and are beginning to dress.

A manservant brings them warm water in a copper basin: no need to go out to a trough in the yard. But they do not wash quite so thoroughly as the gentry; they have not been brought up to consider grubbiness a disgrace to young men of their birth. Soon they are putting on their clothes.

Ralph has recently received the tonsure of a clerk and it would be wrong for him to wear bright colors. Over his white linen shirt he puts on a tunic and matching hose of gray wool. His outer garment is a dark gray *garde-corps*, not a surcoat. Its very long sleeves dangle while his arms come out through holes below the shoulder; the hood lying flat on his back has been folded so elegantly that it would be a shame to disarrange it, like unfurling a smart umbrella. He is down from Oxford for the Long Vacation—the summer vacation. In his dark clothing with its hanging sleeves and ornamental hood we may already see the prototype of the academic gown. But though his clothes are somber he is the elder son of a wealthy man; all is cut from the finest broadcloth and dyed accurately to exactly the right shade.

He combs his hair away from the crown of his head to display his new tonsure; for the same reason he does not wear a coif. His shoes are of thin black leather, coming well over the instep to show that he is more accustomed to riding than walking. His girdle and wallet, worn under the *garde-corps*, are also of plain black leather; his small but sharp eating knife is carried in a horizontal sheath just above the wallet.

Roger will soon be joining his father's business, and his dress as a wealthy young merchant is much more elegant and striking. His shirt also is of fine white linen, the smartest material for town wear. In this hot weather he wears a tunic of lightweight green English worsted. His long sleeveless surcoat is of scarlet Norwich cloth, valued by the customs officers of Venice as the most expensive woolen fabric in the world. His dress is completed by an embroidered coif, green hose, and soft shoes of scarlet cloth laced on the inner side, not over the instep. His girdle is of stamped leather, the large wallet on the right balanced by a dagger nearly as big as a short sword.

In truth Roger is shockingly overdressed for a working day. But he is not a gentleman by birth; neither is his father, so there is no one to tell him when to stop. Any knight who sees him in the street will despise him.

Anne wears a simple gray kirtle, kept in at the waist by a girdle of red silk cord. Her mantle lies open in front, fastened from shoulder to shoulder by a silver chain. It is a rather sad brown; but the lining is edged with beaver fur, which makes it a very smart garment indeed. The unmarried daughter of a burgess ought to dress quietly, but there is no harm in showing discreetly that her father is very wealthy. Her hair hangs loose down her back; over it lies a white veil, resting on her shoulders without a wimple to display her young throat. Her shoes and hose are sober and dark. She carries no wallet at her girdle, which looks unpretentious and at the same time implies that there will always be a servant within call. She shares her little bedroom with her attendant, the middle-aged nurse who looked after her when she was a baby.

John White dresses throughout in sky blue, tunic, surcoat, and hose all of the same shade. The effect is somber and rich, for that color cannot come from native woad but must have been made with dye imported from the Mediterranean. His blue hat is round with a turned-up brim, on the lines of a modern bowler. He wears it directly on his head, for as an indoor man he needs no coif to keep his hair from blowing about.

Dame Joan wears a kirtle and mantle of plain black; her wimple and veil hide most of her face. She does not care for striking clothes, and wishes that bystanders would not point her out as the wife of a famous merchant.

The family is now assembled in the hall. They line up in a little procession: first the two boys, then Anne, then their parents. Behind each walks a personal servant carrying a little kneeling-cushion, and in front are two serving-men. In this order they set out to walk eighty yards to the parish church, as though they were beginning a dangerous journey.

The parish churches of London always had a full complement of clergy, even though there were a hundred of them within a square mile. The Whites can be sure of hearing Mass before beginning the work of the day. They drop in very frequently at their parish church, especially the women. It is a recognized meeting place, one of the few places where a respectable woman may see her neigh-

141

bors. Preachers complain that the women squatting on their heels at the back of the church are often too busy chatting together to say their prayers. Sometimes a devil can be seen filling a large sack with their idle gossip; he is an inferior and put-upon devil named Titivallus, and he is not allowed to return to his comfortable corner of Hell until the sack is full.

After Mass the Whites return home in the same formal procession. In the hall they munch standing their breakfast of fancy bread and watered wine, and then separate for the work of the day. Anne and her mother supervise the housekeeping, Roger visits the stable; Ralph, who is on holiday, strolls out to look up his friends. John White goes to his tall standing desk in a corner of the hall, where he may consult with his clerks.

Unlike most of the characters described in this book, John White is not doing what his father did before him. Wholesale international trade is a novel calling, only just begun to be practiced in London; though in Italy there are banking houses nearly a century old. He is a very daring man, habitually running risks which would appall a brave knight. But he has to feel his way through an unfriendly world, where the law gives him little protection, and where public opinion, if it were sufficiently stirred to notice him at all, would certainly disapprove of him.

The men of the Middle Ages could not see that wholesalers and financiers fulfilled any useful function; it was believed that anyone who made a living by buying and selling must be cheating someone. Ideally the producer should sell direct to the ultimate consumer; and he ought to sell in open market at the prevailing price, which ought never to fluctuate very greatly. This price should be governed by the cost of production, leaving the producer enough to live decently without getting scandalously rich, rather than by the forces of supply and demand. There was a stringent law against forestalling, which is buying goods on their way to market with the object of cornering the supply; and another against regrating, which is buying goods in the market and selling them again at a higher price in the same place.

It was agreed that a trader who imported foreign wares—wine, incense, silk—might add the cost of transport to the price at which he had bought them. Since he would be exposed to many dangers from thieves and shipwreck, his profit on a successful transaction should be high enough to cover his inevitable losses. But it was the general opinion that these imports should be kept to a minimum, since otherwise silver would leave the country; and it was obvious that the more silver there was in a country the more prosperous it was.

It is on the whole better that imports should be brought in by foreigners, who can be kept in order. A foreigner cannot plead before an English law court; he is in England on the King's sufferance, and the King may do what he likes with him. He will certainly not be permitted to take away the money for which he sold his imported luxuries. He will be compelled to buy English goods with it.

The Church also interferes with commerce. There can be no moral objection to fair exchange, but investment is a different matter. Since usury is sinful no interest may be charged on a loan. In theory any Christian is entitled to risk his money on the chance of gaining more, say by betting; but the idea of productive investment was not understood. If you have put up the capital for a trading venture you ought to be satisfied when you get your money back.

When John White was young there was an export trade in English wool, but it was run almost entirely by foreigners. Italians or Flemings bought the wool from flockmasters while it was still on the sheep's back, and what they did with it afterward was a matter between them and the King. The men of Bordeaux brought French wine to England. They were not exactly foreigners, since their ruler, the Duke of Aquitaine, was also King of England; but their trade was taxed and regulated in Aquitaine, and did not concern Englishmen.

But nearly twenty years ago the present King, then heir to the incompetent Henry III, was made Duke of Aquitaine in his own right. Prince Edward began to take an interest in international commerce. He levied a uniform import duty, so that wine merchants could calculate ahead. The total sum of this duty might also be estimated in advance. It was soon pawned to a syndicate of Italian bankers, who advanced a lump sum to the King and in return collected the duty for themselves. By the time he reached the throne King Edward I had learned that international trade was a valuable source of royal revenue, which enriched his country instead of impoverishing it.

John White had been born a hereditary member of the guild of vintners. Only vintners might sell wine in bulk, and there were not very many of them. That gave him a start in foreign trade. For a year or two everything went well with him until he had money to spare. He branched out into the wool business, riding all over southern England to buy small clips before they were shorn, selling in bulk to Italians who sent the raw wool to be spun and woven in Flanders.

All this was legitimate, but no way to make a fortune. Presently he began to take chances with the law. Italian merchants, debarred from suing in an English court, paid him to collect their debts for them. He did this by pretending that the debt was due to himself, a native Englishman; that was the crime of *coverture*, lending his nationality to cover a foreign trader. He might have been severely punished if the deceit had come to light.

From buying wool in advance to making temporary loans in money was not a very great step. Many perfectly solvent landholders were anxious to borrow ready money, for the dowry of a daughter or to pay a relief; and there were no legitimate moneylenders anywhere in England.

Ever since the Norman Conquest Jews had been lending money at usury. They had no standing in the law courts, and could not sue for their debts; neither could they hold land even though it had been pledged as security for a loan. But all the Jews in England were the personal servants of the King. The King collected their debts for them; in return he taxed them at his pleasure.

However, King John, the grandfather of the present King, took so much from the Jews that they could barely make a living; and his rebellious subjects lynched them, plundered their homes, and burned the notes of hand they had lodged in royal castles for safekeeping. Under Henry III a group of Jews in despair sought baptism. As Christians they might not carry on their old trade. No one knew what to do with them, but the pious King was delighted; at his own expense he lodged them in a college between Westminster and London. As they died out they left no successors, and their hostel stood empty. Since it was near the law courts it was used to house legal records, under an official known as the Master of the Rolls. It is now the Record Office in Chancery Lane.

By the 1270s the Jews of England were too poor and oppressed to do much moneylending, though they were not finally expelled until 1290. The only other financiers with large resources behind them were the crusading Knights of the Temple. It had long been the custom for English crusaders to pay over money to the Templars in London, and draw on it at any Templar castle in the Mediterranean. That was how King Edward had financed his own crusade, when he was still heir to the throne. But the Order of the Temple is now in decline. Nobody trusts Templars any more, and young Ralph White will live to see them suppressed and their leaders unjustly executed.

John White found that many wealthy landholders were eager to borrow his money. Of course he did not charge interest. Usury was not only a sin and a crime; but such disgusting behavior would have outraged the self-respect of a proud vintner of London. It was perfectly legitimate, however, to buy wool for delivery two years hence at a lower price than that summer's clip.

Within fifteen years John White had become very wealthy indeed. The fair profit on any successful transaction was enormous, because so many transactions could go wrong. He happened to be lucky. No importer in Flanders or Brabant refused to pay and left him to whistle for his money, unable to sue in a foreign court; the King did not prohibit all exports just when he had a cargo waiting at the docks; ships carrying his goods were not captured by pirates, or by honest foreigners exercising their legal right of reprisal because some other Englishman owed them money. On this fine August morning John White is very rich and very busy.

Like other thirteenth century merchants with capital to spare he trades in anything and everything. The foundation of his business is the export of wool to the Low Countries, balanced by the import of wine from Gascony. In addition he exports finished cloth, though of course only the best quality is costly enough to bear the cost of carriage. English broadcloth is of prime quality. The pieces, 26 yards long by 2 yards wide, are woven on two looms by two weavers working side by side; Italian tailors are eager for it. English worsted is the best wear in hot weather; the Knights of St. John, in their

148

faraway island fortress of Rhodes, order summer mantles made from it. Norwich scarlet, as worn by young Roger White, is valued at thirteen shillings and fourpence a yard at a period when the wage of a knight is two shillings a day; a length of it made a suitable present from King Henry III to the Sultan of Damascus.

The mainstay of John White's import business is wine, the appropriate trade for a London vintner. A few English religious houses still grow their own grapes and make their own wine, as had been more general a thousand years earlier when perhaps the climate was more genial. But these home vineyards are maintained chiefly so that sacramental wine will be available even in time of war with France. Anyone who drinks for pleasure wants a foreign wine. Since there are neither glass bottles nor corks the wine of Bordeaux is not yet a fine claret; it is the ordinary table wine which every gentleman drinks every day.

Choice wines come from farther afield. Malmsey probably took its name from the town of Monemvasia in the Peloponnesus; but though it was made from Greek grapes it reached England in Venetian ships, and was generally supposed to be a product of Italy. There was a similar misconception about the currants which came from Corinth. Venetians were the great long-distance importers. They had an understanding, rather shocking to their fellow Christians, with the infidel rulers of Egypt. In Alexandria their ships loaded cotton and muslin, spices from the Far East, alum from Asia Minor, monkeys and parrots from India. For generations the East saw Venice as the great source of European goods. In several Oriental languages a firearm is still *bundook*, the thing from Venice.

Every year a Venetian fleet undertakes the long voyage down the Adriatic, westward by Sicily and Gibraltar through seas infested with infidel pirates, then northward by the Bay of Biscay to the Channel. Its goal is the great international mart of Bruges, but often it calls at Southampton on the way. Yet a large proportion of Venetian trade does not come by long sea voyages. Another busy trade route comes by the Brenner Pass and down the Rhine to the fairs of the Low Countries. Except for the crossing of the Alps, by an easy and well-guarded pass, this is a level journey and much of it can be made by water. It is safer for fragile goods than the boisterous sea; and is the easiest, though not the quickest, way for an English clerk to get to Rome. The speediest route from England to Italy is by France and Provence over the western Alps, but only a stout traveler in a hurry would face its dangers.

Venice is the chief source of exotic goods, but many imports come from Spain: soap, sugar, oranges, above all Cordova leather. London has its own guild of cordwainers, who claim to dress leather as well as any Spaniard; but it is generally agreed that the true product of Cordova is superior to any local imitation.

A merchant of London, especially if he keeps on good terms with the Italian bankers, may trade in all these Mediterranean commodities. He may buy part of a cargo before it leaves Italy, or take a share in the ship which carries it. But he may buy only in London, as an importer, goods which reach London by the other great medieval trade route, from the Baltic by way of Flanders. Hansas, syndicates of north German and Flemish traders, control this business closely, and allow no competition. The Hansa of Bruges regards the English market as so important that no citizen may hold office in his municipal government until he has endured the appropriate period of exile in the Hansa's London hostel.

All this thriving international trade was conducted on a basis of tiny silver coins. Silver was the only measure of value; gold, though it might be coined, was a commodity like any other. Surviving records mention casually enormous quantities of silver. For example, in 1296 King Edward arranged that one thousand pounds a week should be made available in Newcastle for the pay of his army on the Scottish border, and it is hard to see how this could have been done except in the form of 240,000 silver pennies. But soldiers must be paid in hard cash. Merchants avoided as much as they could this dangerous and costly transport of barrels of small coins.

On his standing desk in the hall John White has a list of the bonds he keeps in a locked chest in his solar above. When he sells wool to the Sienese bankers they give him sealed drafts instead of cash. With these drafts he may buy goods in any market in Christendom, from Hamburg to Messina; for the bankers of Siena, financial agents to the Papacy, have branches in every country which owes obedience to the See of Rome. Every important merchant has his personal seal, internationally

151

known, and his bonds pass from hand to hand until eventually they reach Bruges. Italian bankers settled in Bruges run a clearinghouse, where in the end these bonds will be cashed and the drawer will have to pay up. But he need not pay cash; unless his business has been very unsuccessful he will settle largely in the bonds of others, for which he has sold his own goods.

It is a sophisticated and convenient system, which avoids the danger of transporting barrels of silver over unguarded roads. Like any other system of credit, it has its dangers. One trouble is that the world of trade is wider than the world of news. A merchant in Bergen or Naples may have failed long before news of the crash can reach Bruges, and in the meantime his bonds will be used to settle debts between third parties. Through no fault of his own the most prudent trader may find himself with a strongbox full of worthless paper.

Since everyone would have been shocked at the suggestion that these bonds should bear regular interest, bankers covered themselves by accepting them at less than their face value. That gave scope for individual skill. If John White demands too big a discount no one will trade with him; if he asks too little he will lose money. He must use his own judgment. Every deal is concluded in private, and there are no published lists of stock exchange prices.

This intricate commercial world is quite outside the comprehension of feudal rulers, who see wealth as consisting only in silver or land. Merchants must draw up their own rules, and enforce them without aid from the state. When English justice tried to interfere in commercial matters it usually made a hash of it. There was a famous lawsuit between James le Roy of Dixmude in Flanders and John de Redmere of Lincolnshire; they had been trading in partnership, exchanging English wool for spices and cloth from the Flemish market, until by 1274 John the Englishman owed James the Fleming two hundred marks (one mark = 180 pennies or thirteen shillings and fourpence). James brought suit in a special English court, set up to settle such matters after four years of interrupted diplomatic relations between England and Flanders. John agreed that the debt had been owed, but claimed that he had paid it and produced a receipt bearing James's seal. James said the receipt was a forgery. The judges compared the receipt with other admittedly genuine seals and pronounced it valid. James was committed to prison for maintaining a false claim on oath.

Other merchants of Flanders protested to the King, and in 1278 the case was reopened. The judge appointed to try it was specifically ordered to consult experts on commercial custom. These all agreed that in a conflict between sworn testimony and a sealed document the sworn testimony should prevail, since seals were easily copied or stolen. By the custom of the merchants James was in the right. John was ordered to pay the two hundred marks, and since he could not pay it at once he was compelled to produce before the shire court of Lincoln pledges who would guarantee payment.

Yet it appears that James never got his money. In

1284 he was still pressing for payment of this debt which had been incurred before 1270. He complained that the sheriff of Lincoln, John's personal friend, would neither distrain on John's land nor arrest the neighbors who had stood pledge for his debt. All James got out of this effort to collect money due to him was a term of imprisonment for perjury.

He could not have come into court at all if a commission had not been set up to inquire into English commercial dealings with Flemings, because for four years all intercourse had been suspended. The old Countess Margaret of Flanders had seized all English merchandise in her dominions because she claimed that King Henry III owed her money. In reprisal the English government prohibited the export of English wool to Flanders, and then made a substantial revenue by selling exemptions from its own rule. In 1274 trade was resumed, but the dispute was not settled until 1278. Countess Margaret, though impetuous, had acted completely within her rights. It was recognized international law that if a foreigner owed you money you were entitled to seize compensation from anyone else of the same nationality; if French pirates captured your ship you might in revenge capture any other French ship.

King Edward, by the way, was famous as a friend of merchants. If this was the best he could do for James of Dixmude we can see that international trade was a chancy way of earning a living.

But if a merchant could steer clear of heavy-handed feudal rulers the profits were enormous. So far John

White has guessed right, and has suffered no undeserved calamities. He is very rich indeed.

Young Roger is learning to help his father; but at ten years of age he is not trusted with the tricky business of sealing and accepting bonds. His place is in the stable, not in the counting house. He passes the morning in looking at mules and packponies, and chatting to grooms about the state of the roads and the activities of brigands in the Chiltern Hills; then he walks down to the harbor beside the Tower of London to see what foreign ships have come in and to learn the latest news of pirates. He likes to chat with foreigners, for it gives him an opportunity to display his skill in the foreign language.

To young Roger, as to many merchants, there is only one foreign language. At home he speaks English to his parents, but he hears so much French spoken all around him that he has picked it up without consciously learning it. Flemish is so like English that it seems to be rather another dialect than a foreign tongue. *The* foreign language is the speech of sailors from the Mediterranean, a mixture of Provençal and Italian and Spanish. It is current throughout the Levant, so that infidels suppose it to be the language of all Western Christians. To Moslems all Western Christians have been Franks since the days of Charlemagne. Until the end of the eighteenth century this international tongue will remain current under its Italian name, the *Lingua Franca*.

Meanwhile Ralph has collected a group of clerks who knew him before he went up to Oxford a year ago. They are all on holiday at the same time, in theory because they will be wanted to help with the harvest at home. But Ralph and his friends are too grand to reap grain with their own hands, and few of them come from landholding families. Since they have nothing else to do they are strolling through Smithfield outside the walls.

At Smithfield there is always something to see, even on the morning of a working day. Horsedealers are showing off hackneys, and one man is trying to sell what he claims to be a genuine trained destrier. Enough idlers have collected to start a game of football, and young squires from the noble houses along the Strand and at Westminster are practicing at the quintain. There are tumblers and jugglers.

Anne helps her mother about the house, and seizes every chance to go out into the street on errands. She visits the butcher and the baker, for in London bread and meat may be bought retail on any day and you need not wait for a weekly market. With her mother and several servingmen for escort she goes down to the riverside to inspect the cookshops. They buy a new kind of pie for their own cook to copy at home.

It is sad that the cookshops of London lie in rather a rough quarter, infested by the touts who prey on sailors; for the cookshops are one of the most famous sights of the city. In these shops you can buy a complete meal, and either eat it on the premises or have it sent home. The dishes on offer are worthy of a nobleman's table; there is even venison, though it would be tactless to ask where it came from. Nowhere else in England will you find such eating houses; in provincial taverns and beer-shops they do not serve food. You would not find another genuine eating house this side of Paris.

There are of course dozens of other shops where it is fascinating to linger: a whole row of goldsmiths in Cheapside, tailors and mercers and grocers. Some of the grandest shops are very small; there may be just a counter flush with the street, where customers stand talking to the shopkeeper within. Nowhere will Anne see a surcoat or kirtle displayed for sale. Since all dressmaking is done by hand there is no saving in buying ready-made clothes; the poorest Londoner, unless he wears cast-offs, has his tunic and hose made to measure.

At midday the family assemble for dinner in the hall. A trestle table has been brought in, with two long benches. There is no dais for a high table, and since no one present is of gentle birth there is no need for a ceremonial saltcellar. But everyone in the house knows his place. The Whites sit at one end, then their clerks and next their foremen, with the ostlers and servingmen and maids lower down. Grubby kitchenmaids bring in the food from the kitchen in the yard. There are no well-dressed pages, no screens to separate the scullions from the diners.

But the food served to the Whites is as good as you would find in a great castle: quantities of beef and mutton and white bread, and an abundance of fish. This fish is a luxury, though a modern gourmet might not

157

value it. In the Middle Ages sheer size was esteemed above delicacy of flavor; if the men of those days could have come by a dead elephant they would have roasted it whole and held it to be a dish fit for an emperor. Whitebait and trout and lobster are scorned as small; sturgeon is reserved for the King and porpoise for the Queen. At this dinner the most highly regarded dish is a large and hideous dogfish.

The custom of the whole household dining at a common table is inconvenient for a merchant, who cannot discuss his business before such a large company. John White must observe the custom, or his clerks would be offended; but he envies what he has heard of Italy, where the rich are beginning to dine by themselves in rooms set apart for the purpose. As soon as he has finished eating he moves with his family to the parlor on the upper floor. There he sits in a chair before a small table covered with an Oriental carpet; his family sit on stools, but all share the excellent wine, worthy of a vintner of London, and the sweetmeats that go with it. Here they may talk undisturbed.

Roger tells his father the latest news about traveling conditions. Roger is learning the ins and outs of a business which he will presently inherit. That was one of the most striking differences between town and country life. Agricultural land went to the eldest son and no argument about it; a father could not disinherit him even if he wanted to, though he might make provision for daughters and younger sons. A burgess in a town was expected to leave his fortune to his youngest son, though he had rather more latitude in making his will. The theory behind this custom of "borough-English" was that most burgesses were craftsmen. By the time an elderly burgess died his elder sons would have finished their apprenticeship and set up for themselves in their chosen craft; but the youngest son, who might still be in his cradle, would need the stock in trade to support himself while he learned a craft.

John White may dispose of his house as he pleases. He may sell it while he lives or bequeath it to a stranger without seeking permission from any overlord. He holds it by burgage from the city of London, which is regarded as a corporate lord.

There is no craft he can teach Roger, and no need for a formal apprenticeship; though to safeguard his son's citizen-right he has had him enrolled as a vintner apprenticed to his father. What Roger must learn is rather "know-how" than a craft or trade. By watching his father at work he may learn when to trust and when to insist on security; by noting the information that comes into the counting house and how it is used he may learn when to buy, when to sell, and when to wait for prices to settle. His most valuable asset will be the friendship of his father's old associates, as is always true when an heir succeeds to a family business.

While Roger and his father are discussing the prevalence of piracy, and whether it would be wiser to ship their wool to Bruges or to sell it to Venetians at South-ampton for a lesser price and no risk in transit, Ralph has been dazzling his sister with stories of his adventures in learned and wicked Oxford.

He came home in July, at the end of the summer term; but he still has not finished his stories, for this is his first visit home since he went up as a freshman in October. Only in the Long Vacation is there time for travel; the brief holidays at Christmas and Easter are passed in Oxford.

At the age of seven Ralph was sent to a London grammar school—actually a secondary school where boys are taught Latin grammar and rhetoric in preparation for entry in the University. He soon decided that he would be a clerk. He is not in love with learning; he does not intend to devote his life to the study of philosophy or divinity. He has found that he can manage easily the tools of the clerkly trade, reading and writing and speaking on a theme; and has made up his mind to win money and influence by his skill. Lawyers seem to get more money for less work than any other class of professional men, and he hopes to become a lawyer of the latest and most fashionable kind.

Before he was seven he had been taught to read and write, and to do simple sums with the aid of an abacus. Like his brother and sister, he had been taught by the clerks in his father's counting house. When he went to the grammar school of St. Paul's Cathedral he was able to begin straight away on Latin. Ralph's schooling cost his father nothing. The master, his orthodoxy vouched for by the Bishop of London, is paid from the common fund of the city; the building is provided free of charge by the chapter of the Cathedral. But the pupils must provide their own writing materials and these are expensive.

That was the common pattern of medieval schooling. Teachers were paid, and buildings provided, by some public authority as a public service, and the teaching was closely supervised by the Church lest heresy creep in. In London there were three grammar schools, and there was at least one in every cathedral city or prosperous market town.

If all this was provided free of cost to the parents we may wonder why every medieval boy did not receive a secondary education. The answer is that schooling in the thirteenth century, though free, was hard to get and most unpleasant while it lasted. The number of places was limited, and apparently the master might fill them as he wished. Perhaps if he could not find enough clever boys he would not be averse to accepting a tactful present to fill a vacancy, but all that we know of these schools has come down to us in the biographies of saints and scholars who were chosen for their early promise. Nicholas Breakspear, the future Pope Adrian IV, was educated free of charge; and so probably was Tom Becket, the future Archbishop of Canterbury.

Boys would continually drop out of grammar school, either because their parents needed their labor or because they could not endure the hard life of learning. To learn a craft took a seven-year apprenticeship, and if a boy was to earn his living by twenty-one he must leave school at fourteen. If he was stupid, or even slow, he would not be able to bear the incessant beating.

Every lesson followed the same pattern. The master would dictate in Latin from his precious textbook, probably the only book in the school. The boys would take down what they had to learn; and then learn it, without assistance or explanation from the master. Probably they would learn the whole lesson by heart. The master would question them individually, in Latin, and anyone who could not answer in the exact words of the lesson would be beaten across the shoulders with a stout stick. Beating was the characteristic activity of a schoolmaster; anyone who wanted to depict a school in a painting or carving would show a grown man beating a boy as the handiest symbol of education.

Latin was the only language permitted, in lessons or in casual conversation; a boy overheard speaking in English or French would be beaten for it. In some Scottish schools at the present day teachers are addressed as "Domine" (master) as a reminder that the question which follows ought to be in Latin. So long as the master stuck to his book he need not understand what he was teaching; certainly he did not worry about keeping the interest of his pupils. Lessons continued all the hours of daylight, with an interval for the boys to go home to dinner. There were no organized games, no recreation except on Sundays and holidays.

Ralph stuck it out for six years, until he was thirteen. By then he could think and speak in Latin as easily as in English, take dictation at speed and read back what he had written, and repeat, without necessarily understanding them, the complicated rules of Latin grammar and an even more complicated catechism. Stubborn endurance had got him through. So far no one had asked him to think; that would come later.

In his fourteenth year his father sent him to Oxford. For the first time John White must spend money on the education of his son. There was a year's board and lodging to be paid in advance to the master of his hall of residence; after Ralph has looked around a bit and taken advice from senior scholars he must enroll among the pupils of a Regent Master, who will demand a stiff fee. But the standard of living at Oxford is not high. His hall gives him a place to sleep, a dinner, and in very cold weather a fire; if he is in funds he may buy himself breakfast and supper, but many undergraduates manage on one meal a day. He wears the same clerical *garde-corps* everywhere, and he is forbidden to frequent taverns.

As soon as he arrived in Oxford he received minor orders and the tonsure from one of the Irish bishops who lurk about the University to the annoyance of the Bishop of Lincoln in whose diocese it lies. English bishops are always complaining about the invasion of their sees by these penniless exiles. The trouble is that England has too few bishops and Ireland too many, and the Irish bishops are often driven from their native land by civil war.

Ralph cannot be blamed for this irregularity. He must be tonsured if he is to study at the University, which has no room for laymen; and he cannot reach the Bishop of Lincoln, who lives far off and is very busy.

At fourteen years of age he is one of the younger

163

undergraduates; but in the lecture rooms he will find plenty of contemporaries. The full course, from freshman to Master of Arts, may last anywhere up to twenty years, and ambitious scholars matriculate young.

The University is not interested in the discipline of undergraduates, but Ralph will be under authority. As a Londoner he belongs to the southern "nation," which includes all Continental students and Englishmen born south of the river Trent; the northern "nation" takes in all Scots and Irish, which makes it nearly equal in numbers. The officers of his "nation" will supervise his behavior in public places. The master of his hall is responsible for his conduct indoors, and for his health; this master may beat him for boisterous behavior, or expel him for a grave fault. His studies are supervised by the Master of Arts he has chosen as his tutor. For the last forty years the University has made it a rule that every undergraduate must choose a tutor, who will see that he does not waste his time.

Ralph had better avoid the shops, even though he is the son of a wealthy merchant. The University posed a novel problem to the town. Never before had more than a thousand clerks been congregated in one place, producing nothing and earning nothing, and buying their food in the open market. Naturally the townsmen put up their prices; naturally the clerks, who had never heard of supply and demand and would have disapproved if it had been explained to them, felt that they were being cheated. The result was frequent town-and-gown riots, in which senior members of the University sometimes rang the bells of St.

Mary's to rally their forces in open war against the thieving shopkeepers.

Instead of reading books, which are expensive manuscripts, Ralph must learn by hearing lectures. These are more exciting than the lessons in the grammar school. Every lecturer tries to advance a new point of view, to make a novel contribution to knowledge; the student is not expected to believe everything he hears; he must choose among conflicting opinions.

For the first time in his life Ralph is expected to think for himself. Above all, he is expected to argue. The men of the thirteenth century had complete confidence in the human mind; they believed that a reasonable man who followed the laws of logic must inevitably arrive at a correct conclusion. A very few fundamental tenets of theology, the nature of the Trinity and so forth, could never have been discovered by the unaided human reason; but God had revealed these truths to His Church.

It is Ralph's duty to listen to disputations in the schools. These disputations are sometimes mere technical exercises, in which a scholar shows his skill by proving, according to the forms of logic, a proposition which he knows to be absurd. But more often than not a serious problem was concealed under deliberately farfetched terms of reference. That it was once disputed how many angels can dance on the point of a needle seems to have been an unfounded jibe of the Renaissance. But even this absurd question conceals an important problem, which may be stated thus: Angels are pure spirit—But when they reveal themselves to mortal men they appear to occupy space—Is this space in fact occupied?—Can one angel get in the way of another angel? To a Christian interested in the nature of angels that is a matter worth investigating.

In the early days of the University of Paris some scholars held a mock disputation in a tavern, in which it was concluded that the soul of an archdeacon cannot be saved. For generations afterward that conclusion was quoted, especially by clerks who had fallen foul of an archdeacon, the financial agent and debt-collector of every diocese. But here again a serious question is involved, a question not at all easy to answer: If a man has the duty of collecting money, even though he does not collect it for himself, can he spend all day harrying debtors and remain holy at the end of it?

The arguments that Ralph hears are penetrating, and often lead to valuable conclusions. If sometimes the conclusions are great nonsense, or seem so to our modern minds, that is not usually because of any flaw in the logic but because the disputants began from wrong premises. Here was the great weakness of the medieval method. Argument was based on accepted beliefs, and no one inquired whether these beliefs were in fact correct. If bear cubs are born shapeless, and then licked into shape by their mother, certain conclusions must follow about natural history; if Constantine the Great gave dominion over all islands in the ocean to Pope Sylvester, certain conclusions must follow about King Edward's claim to be Lord of Ireland.

The greatest undecided question, the question which exercised all the best brains of the thirteenth century, was whether the Emperor was the colleague of the Pope or his subject. In practice it had already been decided, by the death of the Emperor Frederick II; to us it seems absurd that a chance-chosen German warlord should set himself up as the equal of the head of the Church. Yet even in the succeeding century the argument was still alive; Dante, with all his wisdom and learning, could persuade himself into joining the Ghibelline faction, which upheld the authority of the Emperor against that of the Pope.

For a year Ralph has been attending lectures and disputations, chiefly in the fields of theology, philosophy, and Roman civil law. If he wants to become a Master of Arts he must continue listening for several more years, until at last he is fit to engage in the public disputation which is the medieval equivalent of final examinations. Once he is a Master he may support himself by lecturing, or by acting as tutor to paying pupils, in any university in Christendom; for every university recognizes the degrees of every other university. That is what most of his fellow students want to do, though only a minority will achieve it. Some will never reach the stage of public disputation; some will fail in their finals; some will pass and yet acquire no paying pupils. In general a very high proportion of the boys who go to Oxford intend to pass their whole lives there, or at some other university.

That is not Ralph's plan. He has conceived a novel and exciting ambition. When he grows up he intends to argue

167

cases as a lawyer in the secular courts. Oxford cannot give him the grounding in English common law which he needs, so after a few years he will leave. At the University he will have learned rhetoric, which is the art of argument, and enough classical history and Roman civil law to give him the necessary background for his study of the King's law.

The civil law studied at Oxford is Roman law as codified long ago by the Emperor Justinian. It is the basic law of most Continental kingdoms, the only code applied in international disputes. The canon law of the Church rests on the same principles. But it has no connection with the law of England, save that it is known to every practicing lawyer and occasionally applied to a case not covered by any English precedent.

As originally conceived, the English legal system had no room for professional lawyers. Every free man was supposed to know the law of his own locality, and to apply it whenever he was summoned to hear suits in his shire court or hundred court. Very grave cases would be judged by the King in person, or by his deputies appointed for the purpose.

The same law was not applied all over England. Kent had a system of its own, very different from the Saxon law of Wessex; the North and East used a law that was as much Danish as Anglian. Feudal custom had affected some districts more than others; though everyone would agree that Norman and Angevin kings had kept in force the good old law of St. Edward the Confessor. The King's writs might alter the penalties for crime and make regulations in police matters; but the law of each shire had come down from time immemorial and ought not to be changed.

During the last forty years the King and his advisers in Parliament have been openly making new law, especially new regulations about the judgment of disputed claims to land. Only an expert can keep track of these changes. As justices in eyre travel from one part of the country to another they are slowly forming a law common to the whole realm, the common law of England. The only way to learn the procedure of this common law is by constant attendance in court.

There is already a class of men who make their living by attending court—the attorneys. They are not advocates, but rather agents for an absent principal. In every county the sheriff must visit each hundred-court three times a year. This circuit of the county is known as the sheriff's tourn. It is the duty of every landholder to be present to meet him. But they cannot all be present every time; a man may hold land in three different shires. A landholder who cannot be present may appoint someone to represent him at the tourn—an attorney. In the beginning this attorney might be anyone trusted by the landholder, sometimes his wife (modern lady lawyers have a long ancestry). But procedure in the court was formal; a charge must be denied in exactly the correct words, a claim made under exactly the right heading. Very soon it was seen that a trained attorney was better than an inexperienced friend.

The attorney was still nothing but a representative. He

might give a promise to pay on behalf of his principal, or make a claim, or assent to a compromise. If he was attorney for several different principals, and frequently in the courts, he began to know the ropes.

Therefore a great man summoned to appear before the King's judges might bring his attorney with him to help in the pleadings. Perhaps the case was complicated, so that even the judge did not at once understand the issue. The judge might recognize the familiar face of the attorney, and ask him to explain; the attorney would presumably know both the law and the facts. Thus the attorney grew into an advocate, making eloquent speeches on behalf of his client.

When the King's judges sat on their bench a space was kept clear before them by a bar at waist level. Plaintiff and defendant stood against this bar, with the spectators behind them. When the judge gave permission for an advocate to address the court he stepped up to this bar; sometimes, as a compliment, he was invited to come within the bar and address the judge close at hand. By the 1270s these new professional advocates, unknown until about thirty years before, were beginning to be called barristers.

Ralph hopes to be a barrister, and is doing what he can to fit himself for the novel profession. His chief difficulty is to find some place where he may learn the common law. There are famous law schools all over the Continent, and a young but promising school at Oxford. But these teach only the civil law of Rome or the canon law of the Church. The fiction is still maintained that every true

171

Englishman is born knowing the law of his race, and therefore no one makes a business of teaching it. Ralph has decided, very sensibly, that a knowledge of rhetoric and civil law will help, which is why he has begun at Oxford. Perhaps he might have got the same preliminary training at Cambridge, but he has never heard of that small local center of learning. In the thirteenth century Cambridge was famous for eels, not for study.

After a few years at Oxford Ralph will leave without a degree and return to his father's house. There he will be only a couple of miles from the village of Westminster, where the King's judges have their headquarters. By attendance in Westminster Hall he will learn the law, as a village boy learns to work in iron by watching the village smith. At the same time his father will pay a practicing barrister to tutor him by expounding the two or three treatises already written on the common law, textbooks which contain the technical dodges of pleading rather than a comprehensive code.

One day a client will hire him as advocate, and perhaps later a judge who appreciates his competence will invite him within the bar. If he does his work well he may be retained by the Crown. If he still gives satisfaction the King may nominate him to fill a place on the judicial bench; and then Ralph White, son of a London vintner, will be as great as any baron in the land.

The new profession of the law offers great opportunities to the intelligent. It is not controlled by the Church, as are the other branches of learning. The nobility have not yet become aware of it, and do not grab all the best posts for their unemployable younger sons—as they are inclined to grab bishoprics unless the King stands firm. Ralph will remain a lay clerk, able to marry if he wishes; for the tonsure without major orders is no impediment to matrimony. There is as yet no fixed course of promotion, so that everything depends quite openly on favor; a very wealthy father is sure to be a help. Never again will Ralph have to work so hard as he worked in the London grammar school; he looks forward to a secure and peaceful future.

All the Whites are men of peace, but as citizens of London they must undergo a certain amount of military training. The city is in itself a corporate baron, one of the most powerful barons in the land: lord of the whole county of Middlesex, collecting its own taxes and paying them direct to the King, maintaining its own peace, expected to play a part in high politics and to furnish a strong contingent to the King's army.

When John White was an alderman one of his duties was to lead the men of his ward into battle. He still keeps at home the hackney and light mail of a light horseman, the appropriate equipment for a rich burgess not of noble blood. The hackney is sound and well fed, for John remembers that at the bloody battle of Lewes, when he was young, he owed his life to the speed of his horse. But though at Lewes the Londoners were badly cut up they may look back on that stern field with pride. They were the only steady infantry in Montfort's army; by drawing on themselves the full strength of young Prince

Edward's forces, they enabled the rebel barons to defeat King Henry III. As a military power London is taken seriously, even by knights of Norman blood and chivalrous prejudice. It is a treasured tradition of the citizens that London has a voice in the choosing of a King of England. Long ago they proved their claim by keeping on the throne their chosen candidate, King Stephen, through nearly twenty years of civil war.

At Lewes the stubborn resistance of the Londoners cost Prince Edward complete defeat and a year's captivity. Unfortunately Prince Edward is now King, and he is not a man to forget the past. London is still a corporate body, with its own financial machinery and its own apparatus of public meetings. But the King is jealous of its right to elect its own mayor, threatening to appoint a civic head of his own choice. If it should come to an open quarrel, London is not strong enough to defy the King. In practice the privileges of the city, though they continue to exist, exist at the King's good will; so that a King pressed for money may compel the citizens to buy these privileges over and over again.

King Edward fosters trade, in so far as he understands it; but he does not like Londoners, and except in matters of business the city must walk very warily.

The walls of London are strong, and manned by plenty of armed citizens; but the circuit is interrupted by the royal castle of the Tower, so that the King's soldiers cannot be kept out. In any case, the city is so populous that a siege would quickly starve it into surrender; though with the Tower in friendly hands its walls may frighten away a raiding army lacking siege equipment.

If there is a muster during the Long Vacation Ralph will parade with a crossbow, a shirt of mail, and an iron helmet. The crossbow is an intricate weapon, made from many little pieces of wood, iron, and horn, which must all be constantly adjusted to keep the tension correct in changing weather; shooting is easy, but maintenance difficult. It is the weapon appropriate to a young burgess, and is especially useful to a merchant since it can be used as well at sea as on land. Roger is beginning to practice with it, though he is still too young to take his place in the muster.

Meanwhile Anne passes the afternoon at her embroidery; though before sunset she goes out, suitably escorted, to buy more silk thread and look in at the parish church for a gossip. Her life is dull, and she may expect a dull future.

There is no interesting or responsible work for a girl in her station of life. A lady of noble birth may find herself in command of a castle during her husband's absence, with the grave responsibility of deciding whether to yield or stand a siege. The wife of a peasant must help on the land, and perhaps knows more about agriculture than her husband. But the wife of a burgess has only to keep house by buying things, not by making them at home; otherwise she must fill her day with churchgoing and the embroidering of useless trifles.

Occasionally Anne has a day out. Whenever a distinguished visitor receives a civic welcome, maidens walk in procession strewing flowers before his horse or stand in some open space to sing verses in his honor. They may even wear a fancy costume, as angels or Amazons or something else appropriate; though in the cause of modesty they will wear their best kirtles underneath.

Soon Anne will marry a husband chosen by her father. Almost certainly the marriage will be one aspect of a complicated commercial deal, and her husband another wealthy merchant of London. She does not regret that she cannot choose her own partner, for such a wild idea has never entered her head. He may be a pleasant young man, who will do his best to make her happy. But it may be better in the long run if she is given to an elderly husband. Then she may look forward to widowhood before she is too old to enjoy it. As a widow she will be head of the household until her youngest son comes of age, in accordance with the custom of borough-English; and she may be able to make a second marriage to please herself, so long as the man of her choice is not wildly unsuitable.

It is a commonplace of the ballads that the young apprentice married his master's daughter, and this sometimes happened in real life. As a rule it was not the result of a love affair. It meant that the old merchant, lacking a suitable heir, wished to take into the firm a junior partner whom he had trained under his own roof, a partner who would in due course take over the business. There is no evidence that the daughter of Alderman FitzWarren was in love with Dick Whittington before the engagement was announced. We must remember that an apprentice might be the son of an old friend and colleague of his master, of the same social standing. The master's daughter would not be leaving the social class into which she was born.

By sunset all work has stopped and the White family are at home. Soon the city watchmen will proclaim the curfew, and after that no one may walk in the street without a valid excuse. The normal excuse was that you were fetching a midwife; whether this was verified depended, I suppose, on the temper of the watchman. In their snug windproof house, with the shutters closed to keep out the breeze, the Whites sit down to supper in the parlor.

At this time of day they are more comfortable than the Earl's family in their crowded and drafty castle. They have a wider choice of food, with all the resources of a great seaport at their disposal; of course they drink good wine, since they import it. They may talk freely, for they will not be overheard by the crowd of underlings who sup in the hall below. The fire in their chimney draws better than the smoky heap of ashes in the castle hall; they burn coal, which gives out more heat than logs. After supper John White and young Roger will sit long over their papers, but they can be sure of staying indoors until morning; there will be no sudden alarm or unexpected gallop after raiders. Everyone feels secure.

In fact they are not secure. Their investments and bargains depend on unknown forces over which they have no control. Tomorrow King Edward may prohibit all ex-

177

ports; or some foreign ruler, annoyed with a single Englishman, may confiscate all the English goods in his dominions. If pirates capture their ships they have no hope of redress; they have no method more trustworthy than common gossip of foretelling the King's policy.

Merchants stick together against the outside world. The city of London makes treaties with other cities, Bruges or Cologne, for mutual enforcement of bargains which would not be recognized by the law of the land. But there are very few merchants in the world, and a great many people who suppose that all money got by trade is got by cheating. Every bit or parcel of Christian land north of the Alps is ruled by some warrior who does not know enough about commerce to help it even if he should wish to do so. Any great man will consider himself personally insulted if a merchant who has money refuses to lend it to him.

Very few merchant houses endured for more than one generation. John White will die rich, for he understands his trade; but if Roger is not ruined by unpaid loans to Edward II, his son will be ruined by the exactions of Edward III at the beginning of the Hundred Years' War with France.

Someone else will take his place. Medieval commerce was such a lottery that its gains tended to be concentrated in a few hands. In London there will always be wealthy merchants, even though their children may not be able to keep their wealth.

## V

### THE FAMILY OF A CRAFTSMAN

In this East Anglian town a row of small houses shelters all the workers in leather, a smelly trade; no grocer or weaver would want to live next door to a leather workshop. But the one tannery, whose stink is even worse, is kept outside the walls by a regulation of the town corporation.

At first light, people begin to appear in the street. Tom Black, a saddler, leads out his family for a hasty visit to the parish church. They are not especially devout and find that hearing a complete Mass, even a low weekday Mass, takes up too much of the morning. But by long habit they can reach the church just in time for the Consecra-

179

tion; they leave five minutes later, at the end of the priest's Communion. There has been no chance for a gossip with the neighbors, but if there had been any startling news they would have heard it; by looking over the congregation they can note who is sick, or away on a journey. It is a pleasant communal way of beginning the day, even if you are not very inclined to worship. Once again it is a fine August morning.

The Blacks dress soberly, as befits their position. Though they earn a living by the work of their hands they are not mere laborers. Tom and his sons, Ralph and Roger, wear blue tunics over woolen shirts. The tunics reach to the knee, slit open below the waist in front; their color comes from that cheap and almost universal dye, woad. The stout cloth hose are of the same color. Brown leather shoes, open over the instep, are fastened with a strap and buckle; they would never do for a long journey, but then they are only meant for strolling on cobbled streets and standing about in the shop. Girdles are also of plain leather, carrying sensible wallets and small sharp eating knives. Since the Blacks wear their hair cut short they do not need coifs; at present they are bareheaded, but if they were going out in the glare of the midday sun they would wear round felt hats with turned-up brims.

Tom's wife Mary wears a kirtle of the same dark blue, though the shift which shows at neck and wrists is made of linen. Her hose are fitted with thin leather soles which do instead of shoes within the house, but to walk to church she wears wooden clogs which save her feet from the puddles lying about the street even in August. As she comes indoors she slips off her clogs and leaves them by the threshold. Her long hair is parted in the middle and bunched in two coils over her ears. A net of thin cord keeps it in place, but, unlike any of the other grown women in this book, she does not cover it with a veil or a kerchief. That proves she is not pretending to be a fine lady, and also that she does not work in the muddy fields like a peasant.

Young Anne is dressed like her mother, except that her hair lies loose on her shoulders, kept in place by a fillet of red wool. Neither of the women wears any ornament or jewel, apart from the copper clasps which fasten Mary's sleeves at the wrist. These are a very ancient fashion, introduced into Britain by the first pagan Saxon settlers; Mary Black inherited hers from her mother, and in this old-fashioned provincial town the wives of a few other burgesses still wear them.

The whole family are dressed in somber workaday clothes, designed to keep out the weather rather than to make the wearer look attractive (though even the cheapest English cloth is neat and soundly woven). They are completely covered except for their faces and hands; so that if you saw them stripped to wash, which does not happen very often, you would be surprised at the whiteness of their skins. They are an indoor folk, wiry but not very muscular. Their life suits them and they are healthy enough. If they were not perfectly healthy they would have died long ago.

The gable of their house faces the street, one of a dozen gables which make up Leatherdressers' Row. The houses touch one another, so that the town seems densely built up; but if you could look down from above you would see more green than roofs within the walls. There are only a few streets in this town: the two ancient Roman roads which cross by the market and explain why a town grew up here, two parallel streets on the east, and one on the west. These streets are indeed lined closely with gabled houses, but behind each house stretches a long narrow plot of land or toft, somewhat bigger than a mere kitchen garden. Behind his house Tom Black has ground enough to grow vegetables for all his family, to keep a sow and chickens, and to peg out the tanned hides from which he makes his saddlery.

His front door opens directly from the street into his workshop, which for most of its length rises to the timbered roof. On either side of the door are unglazed windows, barred with vertical wooden rods of square section set corner to corner as a precaution against thieves. At the street end a wooden floor supports a second story, lit by another unglazed window in the gable. This platform makes a single sleeping chamber for the whole family. At the other end of the hall, beside the door leading to the toft, is a hearth where cooking may be done in very cold or windy weather. But in summer, and on fine winter days, Mary Black prefers to cook on a little mud oven at the back of the toft, where there is no danger that sparks from her fire may lodge in the open timbers of the roof. She cooks with charcoal, or if she cannot get it, with

182

wood. The coal ships from Northumberland do not call at this little port, and as yet no one has attempted to carry such bulky and heavy fuel by road.

Once a year the plaster walls of the house are whitewashed, inside and out; but the supporting beams have been blackened with tar, and, especially at the gable ends, more beams have been used than are strictly necessary, to make a pleasing pattern. The exterior looks cheerful and bright, though simple. Unfortunately there is no way of avoiding the smell of leather; odd snippets of it always litter the workbench, fixed in the earth floor, which runs the whole length of the hall.

As soon as they are back from church the family eat cold porridge from wooden bowls with wooden spoons, and drink small beer. Breakfast is eaten off the workbench, the only solid furniture in the house except for the bed in the loft above. After visiting the two privies in the toft they are ready to begin work. On Saturday night they will wash their faces and hands very thoroughly, in preparation for High Mass on Sunday; during the week they do not normally wash, though they consider themselves cleaner than common peasants.

After breakfast Tom Black takes off his tunic and settles down with a hammer at his bench. He is smoothing the leather covering of a saddle peak over its wooden frame, which is held firm in a vise. He grumbles a bit about the shape of the frame which the joiner has made for him, but it would be wrong to pass judgment on the work of another craft. Though Tom calls himself a saddler and belongs to the guild of saddlers, he does not make the complete article from start to finish at his own bench. The artisans of the thirteenth century believed most strongly in the division of labor. It would be a serious breach of the municipal by-laws, as well as a crime shocking to all right-thinking opinion, for a craftsman to stray beyond his own craft.

A completely furnished jousting saddle, such as he is now engaged in making, calls for the co-operation of four different crafts. First the joiner makes the wooden frame. Then the saddler covers it with leather and does all the tooling and stamping called for by the design. But such a saddle is always bespoke, ordered in advance by a particular customer; it would be rash to make anything so expensive without having a definite buyer in view. The customer will want to display his arms on his personal property, and the painting of these must be done by a member of the painters' guild. When these three crafts have worked on it the saddle as such will be complete. But no customer would order a saddle without a complete set of horse-furniture to match; the bit and stirrups that go with it, anything made from steel, must be made by a qualified loriner. This craft takes its name from the Duchy of Lorraine, as the makers of shoes, the cordwainers, take their name from Cordova in Spain; because in each of these places the skill was first brought to perfection.

But the chief responsibility lies on the saddler. The knight who ordered this new saddle ordered it from Tom Black, and will pay Tom Black when he takes delivery. Tom will then pay the other craftsmen their set fees, which have been fixed by their guilds so that there is little room for bargaining. Tom himself may bargain with the buyer, who does not belong to any guild; and of course he will be the sufferer if something goes wrong and he is not paid as he should be. For part of the time he is a trader as well as a craftsman, though since there are other saddlers in the town he is not free to ask any price he chooses.

Nevertheless he is his own master, earning his living by his own skill and business capacity: a much more independent man than a peasant who must sow and reap with the rest of his village. He may fix his own hours of work, except that he may not work on Sundays and certain other religious holidays. The Church, the corporation of his town, his guild, and perhaps the King, would all punish him if he did that; which is perhaps a good thing, for otherwise competition might drive him into working all the waking hours of his life.

While Tom shapes leather under his hammer his young son works at the far end of the bench. Roger is apprenticed to his father; or rather, he is beginning to learn the trade with a view to apprenticeship later, since the guild will not permit him to be bound by a formal indenture until he is fourteen. Now he pushes wax thread through tiny holes to stitch together two pieces of a saddle flap; his father made the holes with an awl, and as long as he is careful he cannot go wrong. He has taken off both tunic and hose, partly to keep them clean and partly because the house is hot under the August sun.

His mother and Anne have put on their clogs again to

go out shopping. For some days Mary Black has had her eye on a side of bacon, and if she can beat down the pork butcher to a reasonable price she plans to buy it. Bargaining in the shops is her chief amusement. For bread and salt fish and the other necessities of life there is the market twice a week, where the corporation fixes prices and standards of quality, and sends out official tasters of bread and ale to see that their rules are observed.

If trade is slack and the Blacks have no ready money they can struggle along without buying food, thanks to the cabbage, pigs, and chickens in their toft. But if they have money, and can spare the time, it is often cheaper to buy in the market than to eat their own produce. When the corporation fixes the price of food it represents the consumer; to charge more is to break the law, but no one objects to a lower price. If you wait until the evening of market day you may find a peasant woman willing to sell eggs and other perishables very cheap, rather than take them home unsold; this is another advantage enjoyed by the burgess over the peasant, who rarely sees a market.

As she does her shopping Mary Black from time to time wishes that her husband dealt in wares less costly than saddles; if only he were a cobbler, now, she could sometimes swap with the stallholders instead of using money. Money can be a nuisance because it is too valuable to be handy in day-to-day buying. The smallest coin minted is a penny, which is half the daily wage of an unskilled laborer. In her wallet Mary carries a few halfpennies and farthings, made by cutting a penny with a pair of shears along the lines of the cross on the reverse side. But no one seems to cut them quite honestly, and the stallkeepers in giving change always try to make her take something less than an accurate half or quarter. Singly these light fractions of a coin pass current at their nominal value, but one day Tom may have to make a large payment; then the mixed little bits of silver will be valued by weight alone, without reference to the face value of the coins. Dishonest cutting can cost you several pennies in a pound.

On the obverse side, by the way, these pennies bear the head of a crowned king and the legend *Henricus Rex*. This is not, as you might suppose, the head of King Henry III, who died a few years ago. The design has never been changed since it was introduced more than a hundred years ago by King Henry II, King Edward's great-grandfather; Richard the Lion-Hearted and King John never bothered to put their own names on their own coins.

Since at some of the stalls in the market Mary Black buys less than a farthingsworth, she arranges to settle at the end of the month. She cannot read or write, but she possesses the accurate memory of the illiterate; and if she does not trust it she can strike a tally with her creditor, cutting notches on a stick to indicate the amount owed and then splitting the stick down the middle. She keeps one half and her creditor the other, and when she comes to settle the debt the tallies are solemnly matched. All the same, life would be easier if the King would strike coins in some metal less valuable than silver.

The pork butcher is still stubborn about the price of his bacon, so Mary decides that today her family shall dine on bread and cabbage, without meat. The cabbage will be boiled in salt water, after the immemorial English fashion, and eaten hot; only the very poor dine on cold cabbage. She must go home to light the cooking fire. To boil the pot will take only a few sticks, which she can buy by the bundle in the market. On the way she drops in at the baker's for fresh bread, which may be bought daily in a town of this size. Anne carries the shopping; that is why her mother brought her.

Mary Black is an independent housewife, accustomed to laying out her money to the best advantage and planning the family meals without consulting her husband. She leads a more responsible and independent life than if she were married to a peasant or a rich merchant, or even to a country knight; though a countess has greater responsibilities. If she were stupid or lazy her whole household would suffer. But society beyond her household ignores her utterly. To the King and the sheriff and the mayor she is merely the wife of Tom Black, assumed to be under the dominion of her husband in all her actions. If she tried to attend a public meeting of burgesses she would be hustled away by her shocked fellow citizens; there is no guild of housewives. Except in the Church, where some abbesses wielded great influence, and in the higher reaches of the landholding aristocracy, thirteenth century England wasted the capacities of half its population.

189

Anne therefore knows that she will never matter very much, and she is resigned to it. But insignificance has its compensations. Because she will have no dowry and no claim on an inheritance there is no need to arrange her marriage; she may pick a husband to please herself. Already, at the age of twelve, she has an understanding with a handsome young man. They hope to get married within the next four or five years.

It would have been natural for her to choose an apprentice, someone in the same trade as her father. All the workers in leather live in the same street and meet in the same church; left to themselves, many girls marry the boy next door. But the little town, though ten miles up river from the sea, has a busy harbor; and Anne has fixed her affections on a young sailor.

Jack is probably about eighteen years old, though he cannot be sure, for his mother is dead and his father cannot remember the year of his birth. He has just been promoted from ship's boy to able seaman in a seagoing merchant ship. His ship is small, about sixty tons, far smaller than contemporary Italian vessels. From their East Anglian home port the crew of twenty-two seamen, a boy, and a master trade up and down the east coast, from the Forth to London River, and overseas to Normandy and the Low Countries. They do not care to pass the Straits of Dover for fear of the pirates of the Cinque Ports, who have an especial hatred of East Anglian sailors. If these pirates do you an injury it is very hard to bring them to justice. Some time ago King John granted a far-reaching charter to the Cinque Ports, in return for their help in his

war against the French. Their private court of Shipway, staffed entirely by burgesses of the Cinque Ports, has jurisdiction over all quarrels which arise in the Channel; very seldom does it find a Cinque Port ship guilty of aggression.

A few years ago Jack's ship coasted from Flanders northward all the way to Hamburg. It was amply seaworthy for such a voyage, and the coast of the Low Countries is the busiest and best known seaway in Christendom; the ship's owner made a very handsome profit. But the ship's company are very reluctant to go that way again, for during the whole voyage they were dreadfully bullied and harried by ships of the Baltic Hansa. No law or treaty forbids English ships to trade with Hamburg, but the Germans of the Baltic shore think of the trade as their private preserve and frighten away competitors.

The owner cannot order the master to sail to some foreign port against the wishes of his crew; for all seagoing English ships are governed by the Laws of Oléron, which make them into a kind of floating democracy. Since there is as yet no mathematical science of navigation, the master, the only officer on board, is merely the wisest and most experienced of the ship's company. This does not give him the right to hazard the lives of the men who work with him rather than under him. Before a voyage the purpose and route must be explained to the crew, who must then agree unanimously to undertake it. The master directs the common enterprise, and his men must obey his routine orders; though he cannot punish a man on his own authority, but must bring him to trial before a jury of all his comrades. The master may not alter course without the consent of his crew; presumably for the short coastal voyages of those days the ship waited for a fair wind and then made the whole passage on one leg. The clumsy rig does not permit tacking to windward. If a storm arises or they find themselves among dangerous reefs the master must again call a public meeting; any action taken to deal with the emergency must be agreed upon by the whole crew. If the master acts on his own responsibility and a man is lost by it, he will face trial for homicide when he reaches his home port.

Such were the laws codified in Oléron, an island lying off the coast of Aquitaine which was then under the personal rule of King Edward. They governed all the shipping of the Atlantic coast, from Jutland to Finisterre, whether the ships were English, French, or Flemish. But convoys from Venice were reckoned part of the Venetian armed forces, and were under the command of their officers in accordance with the laws of war. Perhaps that was one reason why Venetians made longer voyages.

Since the master of a ship need have no special knowledge of navigation, there is no reason why Jack should not be a master one day. Already he can go aloft to set the one great squaresail which drives his ship, or climb out on the bowsprit to adjust the little headsail which gives her power to maneuver. He is beginning to learn how to manage the tiller; for his up-to-date ship is equipped with a rudder, the latest improvement on the old steering oar. He has heard of the magnetic compass, which has recently come into use in the Mediterranean;

but since his ship is steered along the coast from one landmark to another he will never use that uncanny instrument.

Jack cannot read, though he can recognize a seal or a merchant's mark. But a sailor has nothing to do with buying and selling cargo anyway; his only duty when he reaches port is to deliver his goods to a warehouse. Jack is strong and agile and honest and good-tempered. Unless he is drowned in his youth he will probably end as master of his ship, with a social position quite as good as a saddler's.

Anne cannot read either; in fact, she has never had a day's formal schooling in her life. But she has learned by watching her mother; she can keep house as well, or as badly, as any other wife of a lesser burgess. She may look forward to a pleasant and interesting married life as head of the household while her husband is at sea; but because she loves him she hopes he will be at home most of the time.

When she has carried back her mother's purchases she busies herself in cleaning the house while dinner is cooked. Her father and Roger are still at work, and have scarcely changed their position since breakfast. At last it is dinnertime. Mary Black brings in from the toft steaming wooden bowls of cabbage and loaves of black rye bread.

There is a bowl and a loaf for Ralph, the elder son, but he has not yet returned from the harbor. They begin without him. The sad truth is that Ralph has no trade. He went out, so he said, to look for casual work; if he has been unable to earn any money he may be ashamed to come home to dinner.

Ralph has clumsy fingers and a hot temper, so that he would never make a good craftsman. Before his fourteenth birthday his father arranged his apprenticeship to a cordwainer, who is socially and financially a step above a saddler. But Ralph was too clumsy for the finicky work, and the scarlet leather he spoiled was costly. Naturally his master beat him, until the boy lost his temper and hit back. That was very wrong indeed, as wrong as if he had raised his hand against his father; for an apprentice is in the position of a son of the house, and his master has all the rights of a parent. The cordwainer threatened to take the matter before the court of his guild, who would have punished young Ralph severely and perhaps fined Tom Black. Tom begged his son off, but the apprenticeship was broken by mutual consent.

Tom next arranged that Ralph should go as apprentice to a tanner, though he was nearly over the age for beginning to learn a craft. But Ralph was surly about the disgusting stink of his workplace, and his bad reputation had gone before him. Presently there was another violent quarrel, and Ralph was once more out of a place.

Tom himself could not take him on as an apprentice, for the guild will not permit a singlehanded master to teach his craft to more than one successor; and his successor must be Roger, who as the younger son takes precedence according to the custom of borough-English. Ralph may live at home, but the men of the guild will watch jealously to make sure that he learns nothing about working in leather. Since he cannot read it would be absurd to send him to school, though there are two grammar schools in the town.

So Ralph lives at home and goes out every morning to pick up a few hours' work loading or unloading cargo at the harbor. He is not yet strong enough to carry a man's load, but he is a local boy with a known address and a respectable father who will answer for him; merchants and shipmasters trust him with small valuable packages. For the moment his family is better off than if he were a real apprentice; an apprentice gets no pay beyond his keep, while on most days Ralph earns money and brings it honestly home to his father.

In this thriving town there is a perpetual shortage of casual labor. Every craftsman has been assigned to his trade, and the guilds will not permit him to work outside it; apprentices have no spare time for odd jobs. Usually Ralph finds something to do, if it is only holding a horse for a traveler. But his family worry about him, for his future looks most unpromising. No burgess would permit his daughter to marry an unskilled laborer; probably Ralph will never find a wife. When he is too old for heavy manual labor he will have no sons to support him, and must beg or starve. While Tom Black lives Ralph is known as his son; when his father is dead he will be that dreadful and despised being, a masterless man.

In some ways a masterless man is worse off than a serf. A serf is tied to the soil, and in the law courts his oath weighs little; but his lord values him and has a duty to

196

protect him. No one cares what becomes of a masterless man. Masterless men are the universal scapegoats, suspected of every unsolved crime; if there have been a number of robberies on a particular stretch of road the sheriff may perhaps round up all the masterless men in the district and hang them without trial on the theory that the robbers must be among them. A man in authority is doing his duty of upholding law and order when he flogs any masterless man he encounters. Ralph will avoid that peril as long as he lives in a walled town; masterless men roaming the countryside were the real enemies of good order. But after his father is dead he may be driven forth from the town; the corporation dislikes burgesses who have no visible means of support. The town is an assemblage of many tight little associations, guilds, colleges of clerks, brotherhoods devoted to pious objects; and Ralph will always be outside all of them. As an outsider he will have no rights, no claim on anyone's help, no protector.

Of course his father has made various plans to get this unsatisfactory son of his into some kind of association. The fishermen of the town have formed a hereditary guild, and will not make room for strangers. The deep-sea sailors are not so particular, for few of them marry. But Ralph is clumsy, which is why he cannot learn a craft; if he goes to sea he will fall overboard and be drowned. There are manors in the neighborhood which have room for another plowman and no questions asked. But without oxen or any other equipment Ralph could take up

197

work on the land only on very hard terms; besides, he cannot plow. Reluctantly, since nothing better offers, his father has decided to make a soldier of him.

There is always a demand for common soldiers; in every siege they die like flies of dirt-borne diseases. It is a despised calling, considered by many to be sinful as well as disgraceful. The Middle Ages had a very low opinion of men who fought for hire, without inquiring into the rights of the quarrel; though every man of honor was expected to fight for the lord who held his allegiance. Within living memory of the people we are discussing, France and England were infested with a very terrible set of men, the *routiers*. These were bands of professional mercenaries, who held together even when they were unemployed; in time of peace they robbed along the highway, a habit which gave them their name of "roadmen." Socially they were the lowest of the low, despised even by serfs. In the eyes of the Church they were excommunicate. The law classed them with wild beasts. Anyone who hanged a stray *routier* felt he had performed his good deed for the day.

There are no more *routiers* in England. King Edward hires his mercenaries singly, and sees to it that when they are discharged they do not wander off together in large bands. But the terrible reputation of the *routier* still clings to every mercenary soldier. A knight may fight for wages, since fighting is his craft; a burgess or a free peasant ought to fight willingly when the proper authorities have summoned him to the muster. But a common hired spearman is by definition a scoundrel.

198

In the old days a mercenary might rise to power and fame, though his origin would never be forgotten and the gentry would never treat him as an equal; after King John had been driven from Normandy the *routier* Lupescar governed it for the French, though that did not make him respectable. There was not so much scope for the hired soldier of the thirteenth century, unless he happened to have been born a gentleman. If Ralph could serve mounted and in mail, gallant conduct on the field might win him knighthood and the chance of unlimited promotion. But his father cannot afford to give him more than a spear, a quilted coat known as a hacqueton which will turn a sword cut but not a lance point, and a steel cap. He must pick up a sword for himself, presumably on the battlefield.

Ralph must wait until he is past eighteen. Then, if he presents himself with this equipment at a royal castle, he will be taken on as a foot-sergeant, the lowest rank in the royal army. In the Middle Ages, "sergeant" denoted not a military rank but a way of earning a living; a sergeant was a man who worked for a regular wage, an uncommon manner of life when most people were paid either by piecework or with land. Only the King and a few great lords were rich enough to employ sergeants, who might be of any station in society. Lawyers retained regularly to appear for the Crown in the law courts were known as sergeants at law; the Sergeant at Arms who in the twentieth century guards the Speaker of the House of Commons is a most distinguished gentleman, not a noncommissioned officer with a loud voice.

As a foot-sergeant Ralph will be employed on garrison duty in a royal castle or on police work in lawless country. Probably he will never fight in a pitched battle, for knights are reluctant to slow up their march by bringing infantry with them. But if the whole countryside is called out to resist invasion a trained spearman from the permanent garrison might be put in command of a dozen untrained peasants. From this practice of employing sergeants to instruct untrained volunteers arose the modern meaning of the word.

If Ralph survives the epidemics which always afflict armies he may grow old in the crowded bachelor life of a garrison. There is no pension for a retired sergeant, and when he is past active service he may be turned adrift penniless. But if he has pleased the King he may be quartered on a monastery, with the right to free board and lodging until he dies of old age. Reading Abbey in particular, founded in 1121 by Henry I and therefore regarded as part of the King's own domain, usually had a number of retired sergeants living on its endowments. The monks dared not refuse a request from the King, but they found these elderly veterans awkward companions to live with.

After his dull dinner of greens and bread Tom Black goes back to his workbench feeling that he will be able to provide for the difficult Ralph, if the boy will keep out of trouble until he is eighteen. He must begin to put by money to buy the hacqueton, but then he has been spared the premium which is usually charged for an apprenticeship. A spear is as cheap as a spade, and steel caps are plentiful. Perhaps if he is short of money when the time comes he may borrow from his guild.

The guild of saddlers plays an important part in Tom's life. At the three great feasts of the year, Christmas, Easter, and Pentecost, he walks in procession with his fellow guildsmen to worship at the altar of St. Crispin, the patron saint of leatherworkers. He is expected to attend the funeral of any member of the guild, and the monthly Masses offered for the souls of all deceased members. The guild began, more than two hundred years ago, as a religious association. All the householders in a particular street, who happened also to be workers in leather, formed a burial club. After the guild had been legally recognized by King Richard I its first action, as a corporate body, was to endow its own altar of St. Crispin.

But religious feasts are often associated with eating and drinking; besides prayers, the guild in its early days provided jolly parties. In the eleventh century a guild might be nothing but a drinking club; so that the Anglo-Norman chronicler Orderic Vitalis, explaining the English way of life to Norman conquerors, could write of "drinking dens (*bibitoria*), which in the English tongue are called *gildhus*."

After each solemn guild-Mass there is a guild-feast, with plenty of roast beef and strong ale. Attendance is compulsory; any member who absents himself is heavily fined.

That was how it all began, in the days of St. Edward the Confessor: with a group of neighbors who had united to pray together, and afterward to drink together. Because they were all workers in leather they discussed at their feasts the problems of their craft; there were no leatherworkers outside the guild, so that a resolution passed at the feast would be binding on all the saddlers in the town. Without noticing it, they drifted into becoming a trade association.

The guild's first duty was to protect the livelihood of all leatherworkers. But presently the members became aware of the conflict of interest between the tanners and curriers who want leather to be scarce and dear, and the saddlers, cordwainers, and cobblers who want it to be cheap and plentiful. The great guild of leatherworkers was divided and subdivided to ensure that every member of each guild should be of the same mind. The saddlers are one of these subdivisions. They remember that once they were the comrades of their business antagonists, the tanners. Each of the lesser guilds still venerates St. Crispin, and on his feast day they all go to church together.

By the time Tom Black was out of his apprenticeship the system had been fully organized, in the shape in which it will endure for another two hundred years and more. The saddlers have two principal aims: to ensure that every member earns a good living, and to maintain the high reputation of saddles made in their town. They must see to it that all their members turn out good work. For this reason they insist on a full apprenticeship of seven years before anyone can become a journeyman, so called because he works for a daily wage in the workshop of a master saddler. The journeyman works always under supervision, and provided he has been properly trained he cannot go wrong. The work has been designed by a master saddler; for designing more is needed than a mere industrious apprenticeship. A journeyman will be admitted to the grade of master only after he has shown the guild his masterpiece, something he has made by himself without direction from his employer.

Of course there must not be too many masters, and they must not undercut one another. Within broad limits the guild fixes prices, though for such individual goods as saddles there must be a little room for bargaining. No foreigner trained in another town would be admitted to the guild, and a fellow townsman whose father followed a different trade would be turned down in favor of the son of a saddler if there was no room for both. But the craft is not exactly hereditary. As the prosperity of the town fluctuates, so does the number of master craftsmen. At present there are four master saddlers; though not long ago they were limited to three, and now some journeymen maintain that there is room for a fifth.

By controlling the intake of apprentices the guild tries to limit the number of men working at the trade. But this cannot be done accurately, for no one can foretell how long a fourteen-year-old apprentice will work as a journeyman. He may die young, or leave the town to take private service with some great lord. This question of the right number of apprentices and journeymen divides the masters who rule the guild.

Of the four masters at present working in the town

Tom Black and another employ no journeymen; each has only one apprentice, a member of his family who will one day succeed him. A third master employs two journeymen, and is training two apprentices who will one day replace them. But the fourth has become almost scandalously prosperous; he finds work for seven journeymen, though the guild has limited him to one apprentice. He is a wealthy man, with great influence in the town; if he is consistently thwarted by his fellow masters he can make trouble for the guild.

In many ways his interests conflict with theirs. He wants to widen his market by making agreements with the saddlers of neighboring towns; the other masters are afraid of the competition of these foreigners, who live all of twenty miles away and speak a different dialect. He wants to keep the wages of journeymen as low as possible; the others feel that a journeyman, on his way to becoming a master, ought to live in dignity worthy of a skilled craftsman. But the gravest cause of dispute is that he purposes to employ his journeymen for the whole of their working lives. He has organized his workshop so that each man does more or less the same work every day, until after they have been in his employment for some years they begin to lose the over-all skill which would fit them to be masters. In any case, there is no room in the town for all of them to set up on their own.

Tom Black and his two colleagues see this as something against nature. It is wrong that a man should spend seven years learning a trade merely so that he may work for wages until he dies of old age. Every journeyman ought to have the chance of becoming a master. They cannot bring themselves to oppose a fellow saddler, but they wish that something might happen to diminish the expanding business of this wealthy employer. It is they who want a fifth establishment and their rival who opposes it, claiming that he can handle any increase in demand. They have public opinion on their side; for in the Middle Ages, as in most periods of history, to be rich was to be disliked. But they dare not be too stubborn in their opposition, for anything is better than a split in the guild.

Their wealthy rival is constantly increasing the expenses which fall on a master craftsman. He wants an elaborate High Mass at every service before St. Crispin's altar; he is always proposing lavish guild contributions for civic purposes, such as the repair of the town walls or the cleaning of the streets. Every master contributes equally to these expenses, and Tom Black is sometimes hard pressed to find his share. What would happen if he should fail to pay up is hard to imagine; it is unthinkable that a master should be expelled from the guild, and equally unthinkable that he should remain in it without paying his dues. What the rich man wants, of course, is that Tom should borrow money from him and then vote as he directs in the councils of the guild.

Other guilds in the town are afflicted by these conflicts between rich and poor; for a very wealthy burgess is still a novelty, and ordinary townsfolk do not know how to deal with him. When the guilds became associations of craftsmen it was assumed that all masters would be roughly equal, independent but without money to spare.

Perhaps Tom's guild will elaborate its constitution, setting up an inner council of those masters who are also large-scale employers; perhaps a custom will grow up that lesser men stay away from the meetings and leave all decisions to the great; perhaps the poor will pluck up their courage and vote down the powerful, making regulations against the excessive growth of any one workshop. All these different solutions were adopted by different guilds before the system of guild control of trade began to wither away under the Tudors.

But the most sinister development, something which shocks all the guildsmen of the town whatever their craft, is that the seven journeymen who have no hope of becoming masters are talking of instituting a guild of journeymen saddlers in opposition to their employer. That would be a terrible thing, to bring class conflict into the closed world of the guilds. How could prices and wages be fixed under such a system? It might lead to open competition.

Meanwhile the guild of saddlers remains a going concern, though suffering from the strain of modern life. Tom Black and his household feel safe under its protection. For the guild is also a friendly society. Of course it arranges the funerals and mortuary Masses of deceased members: that was the original purpose for which it was founded. In addition, if a saddler should die poor, whether master or journeyman, the guild will provide for his widow, find husbands for his unmarried daughters, arrange apprenticeships for his sons. No guildsman will die of starvation, or be left to beg his bread in the streets.

Though the guild supervises the craftsman closely it gives a good deal in return; and since it is ruled by the masters no master feels irked by regulations which he himself helped to draw up.

The Blacks know all about their own guild, since Tom helps to govern it. They have not such a clear picture of the town corporation, though they have lived under it all their lives. Tom is proud of being a burgess of a corporate town, and would if necessary fight for it against any exterior power; but in his mind the corporation is "Them," the guild is "Us."

The town has a seal; in law that makes it a person, able to conclude contracts, pay and receive money, sue and be sued in the courts. Not long ago Simon de Montfort commanded the burgesses to send two representatives to his parliament; that set a precedent which King Edward sometimes follows and sometimes neglects. In most years there are two Parliaments, in spring and autumn, and though they often meet at Westminster, handy for the law courts, occasionally they are summoned to remote corners of the realm. Busy men find it a burden to journey to Parliament for an indefinite stay, even though the King normally dismisses them after a week or two. Of course the town pays the traveling expenses of its representatives, and a lodging allowance; but the chosen burgesses find the honor expensive. On the whole the corporation rejoices when the King omits to send them a summons.

On the other hand, a community of craftsmen and

merchants cannot neglect Parliament, since so much of its business is concerned with foreign trade. It is essential that burgesses should attend, to explain to the landholding lords exactly where the shoe pinches. The best solution would be that burgesses should be there at the expense of some other town, while one's own town is left in peace.

To go up to Parliament is a tiresome public duty. No burgess is eager to undertake it. The choice of representatives is never contested, and it would be unfair if the same man were sent twice before every other well-to-do burgess has taken a turn.

Tom Black knows all this. He is proud of his town, and proud that the King should seek its advice. When the chosen burgesses ride off to Parliament he will stand in the crowd and give them a cheer. But as to how they are chosen he knows nothing; certainly no one has ever asked him to vote.

In the same way he is proud of the mayor and councilors who make up the corporation, but not at all sure by what means they reached the positions they occupy. Every Michaelmas there is a public meeting, at which the burgesses are asked to ratify the appointment of the new corporation; but the same faces reappear on the council until old age forces retirement, so that ratification by the whole body of burgesses must be a mere formality.

Of course there has been something of a contest behind the scenes. To be a councilor, still more to be mayor, brings honor and profit to any burgess. The corporation levies a rate for the upkeep of the walls, for the repair of the streets, for the maintenance of the town hall; in addition it apportions among individuals the tallage and other taxes levied by the town's sole lord, King Edward. Anyone who has incurred the ill will of the councilors may find that he has to pay rather a lot.

About a month before Michaelmas the leading merchants meet together in private and share out among themselves the offices for the coming year. In theory, any burgess could oppose the recommended candidates at the annual open meeting, but in practice no poor craftsman would have the nerve to do it.

Long ago, soon after the town had bought its charter by a contribution to the cost of Richard I's crusade, there was a struggle for control of the corporation so fierce that for some years the burgesses hovered on the brink of civil war.

Two groups of guilds were in conflict. On one side were the butchers, bakers, and vintners, together with the brewers and tavern keepers who were not organized into guilds. They made their living by selling to the townspeople, and what they sold was normally cheap; there were few rich men among them. On the other side were what may be called the luxury trades—tailors, saddlers, goldsmiths: small guilds of a few highly skilled masters, whose most valuable market was outside the town walls. One party wanted the town to be as large as possible but was not interested in what happened outside it; the other wanted a small town with a restricted citizenship but plenty of contact with the rest of the country. Was the corporation to encourage immigrants, perhaps enlarge the area enclosed by the walls, and at the same time levy high market dues at the gates? Or should it discourage growth, while inviting all strangers to come in and buy?

The quarrel has been settled, by a compromise which enforces the restrictive practices proposed by both parties. The town remains small and crowded, and it is hard for a newcomer to acquire burgess-right; at the same time exporters are not encouraged in their mildly disloyal dealings with outlanders. Of course substantial dues are levied on anything brought in or sent out, to make life easier for the established burgesses.

As a result anyone born into the right family finds it fairly easy to make a living, though if he tries to grow rich he is hampered by a thousand petty regulations. Yet all the guilds are satisfied, and their leading members have combined unofficially to take over the government of the town. The little men, such as Tom Black, have no say in the conduct of affairs; but neither are they exposed to the competition of more efficient craftsmen.

The policy of each town is to protect its own vested interests; but in the government of the realm there are other factors. Landholders want to buy goods from overseas, and have discovered that they can pay for them by selling wool in exchange; they want to keep imports cheap. The King, though he would like to increase the revenue he draws from customs duties, is normally too pressed for money to take a long view; what matters to him is the income he will receive this year. The interplay in Parliament of all these forces ensures that there will be a good deal of international trade, without cutthroat competition.

In the family of a craftsman, work occupies all the daylight hours of a normal day. Tom Black and Roger will continue to sew leather even after sunset, by the light of tallow candles. They will work until they are too sleepy to concentrate, and then roll into bed without washing. On a working day a craftsman has no leisure at all. But then he enjoys a good many holidays, as many as craftsmen do nowadays, and many more than were granted to the Blacks' descendants in the nineteenth century.

Besides every Sunday, and the greater religious festivals, the town makes holiday in honor of its patron saint. The vigil, the day before the feast, is of course a day of fasting and abstinence; there are no special amusements, but no work is done either, since all good burgesses will be visiting their churches to pray. On the day after the feast everyone has a headache and there is a great mess to be cleared away, so no one goes to work. Some shops remain shut on the day after that, and the custom is spreading. The town is on the way to having a full week of leisure.

In October, all the guilds connected with leather keep a three-day festival in honor of St. Crispin, as other guilds honor their different patrons.

On St. John's Day, in midsummer, the burgesses muster in the market place to practice manning the town wall. Tom Black parades with shield and spear and steel cap, as befits his dignified rank of master. But if a genuine attack threatened he would go on the wall with his crossbow, a deadly weapon in which he is expert. Roger also is learning to manage the crossbow. Poor Ralph, who is not a member of any guild, must fall in with the rabble, carrying only a spear; on the wall he tends a brazier, heating tar to drop on a storming party. Of course, the muster ends with a great feast in the market place.

At Michaelmas the councilors keep open house; if one of them is a saddler he will feast all the other saddlers.

On these holidays the women wear their best clothes and stroll in the market place. To be in a crowd is in itself a treat for them, and since most of the girls are free to choose their own husbands there is ample scope for flirtation.

The Blacks live meanly, in a crowded and dirty house. They are not very clean in their persons. Their food is dull, and they do not always have enough of it. Like all their contemporaries, they will die as soon as a serious illness strikes them. There is still a chance, though it grows less every year, that enemies will sack their town and cut their throats.

Yet each one of them has the chance of a full life, doing interesting work in friendly surroundings, with beautiful churches ready to welcome him and the pleasant countryside within easy reach. The men, at least, may plan their own lives and prosper by their own efforts. They are not gentry, but they call no man master.

212

Two hundred years later, the noble house of the Earl was extinguished in the Wars of the Roses. The family of the country knight was ruined in 1720 by the South Sea Bubble, a speculative scheme to extinguish the national debt. In the eighteenth century the peasant Hills were driven from their holding by an enclosing landlord. The wealth of the merchant Whites endured only for two generations. But in his ancestral town there is still a Tom Black, saddler, whose shop stands in the narrow street that was once Leatherdressers' Row. He feels at home there, and no wonder.

*Note*

For forty years I have been reading about the Middle Ages, and I cannot now acknowledge the sources for everything I have said. But as regards costume I have relied on C. Willett & Phillis Cunnington: *Handbook of English Mediaeval Costume*. London, Faber & Faber, Ltd., 1952.